Fisherman's Knots and Nets

Fisherman's
Knots and Nets

by Raoul Graumont
and
Elmer Wenstrom

Cornell Maritime Press
Cambridge, Maryland

ISBN 0-87033-024-1

Copyright 1948 by Cornell Maritime Press

Library of Congress Catalog Card Number: 48-423

Printed in the U.S.A.

Preface

LONG before the dawn of recorded history, there is evidence that even among the inhabitants of the old Stone Age, primitive man had already begun to fashion crude implements with which to catch fish. The ancient gorge which was used during this period—and continued to be employed in various forms for thousands of years afterwards—was undoubtedly the earliest known type of the present-day fishhook. In later times, during or prior to the first Egyptian dynasty, about 4000 B. C., it is recorded that the first curved hook came into existence. Then finally after a lapse of some two thousand years, we are told, a hook was made to which a barb was attached to prevent the loss of fish which undoubtedly occurred with the earlier type of barbless hook. Thus it would seem that there was some semblance of the modern fishhook as long ago as 2000 B.C.

It is also doubtful that anyone can determine the exact period during which the use of fishing nets came into existence, since this art likewise had its inception in prehistoric times. It is a well established fact that the ancient Swiss lake dwellers were making and employing fishing nets as early as 1000 B.C. However, enough evidence exists—in the written records inscribed on the hieroglyphs contained in the Cairo Museum—to further establish that the making and utilization of fishing nets were accomplished arts as early as the second Egyptian dynasty, thus placing their origin well beyond 3500 B.C. The earliest type of rope to be utilized in netmaking was derived from the fibers of the wax plant. In time, other kinds of plant fibers came to be employed according to their distribution and availability in different parts of the world, and their adaptability for this purpose, such as the coconut fibers from the palm trees in the South Sea area, and a variety of fibrous barks from plants in other areas.

It is noteworthy that, in the course of the evolvement of new ideas, developed out of the necessity of keeping pace with the growing needs for man's survival, the Greeks had already begun to use artificial flies along the rivers of ancient Greece in the early centuries following the time of Christ. After this period there is a lapse of more than a thousand years before we again pick up the threads of civilized progress. As man emerged from the Dark Ages with a renewed incentive toward progressive advancement, there is evidence from a number of sources to indicate that the early procedure of imitating various flies for use as lures was revived, with the addition of certain improvements. However, it was probably not until Izaak Walton's time, in the seventeenth century in England, that the art of creating and employing artificial flies finally became an established practice. From that period onward, up to the present day, there has been a steady increase in the number and great variety of fishing ties, made necessary by the employment of ever-improving equipment, occasioned by the development of more suitable techniques to keep pace with fishermen's growing needs. Fancy marlinespike seamanship and artistic ropework probably reached the peak of their development as the result of an expanded interest among the fishing sailormen of the nineteenth-century sperm whalers.

It is little wonder, then, that down through the countless ages, with the advent of new and increasing accomplishments in the development of fishing equipment and technique, there should have been an equal necessity to develop various forms of knots with which to insure the proper functioning of, as well as the most convenient way in which to handle such equipment. Since it has been our objective in this undertaking to present what we believe to be the most inclusive assortment of fishing ties ever published, we feel that, in so doing, it will add to a wider public interest to show not only the most popular and commonly known varieties, but also to deal with rare and odd ties of varied descriptions, regardless of whether any of these ties are valued for their utility among the great majority of present-day fishermen.

Most fishermen develop special preferences for the particular kinds of knots with which they have become familiar, and are adept in the art of tying and applying them with satisfactory results. Some are inclined to favor a few simple and well-known types of knots that do not require too much perseverance or skill to execute. A few well-chosen knots of this type will usually serve everyday fishing needs, whereas others prefer to acquire a more thoroughly grounded knowledge in the art and use of general knotwork with regard to its proper application in every kind of fishing requirement.

Consequently, the work presented herewith is intended as a general reference guide of an informative nature for fishermen to utilize wherever fish are caught. For this reason we have endeavored to include as thorough a coverage of all the different types of fishermen's knots as are known to have been used from the earliest times to the present day. Anglers and still fishermen, as well as commercial fishermen, will find herein practically every known variety of tie for which they could possibly have any use. Fishing traps and seines are also adequately dealt with. Net-making and repairing are thoroughly explained and illustrated.

Therefore, with the rapidly expanding field of interest in the pursuit of fishing growing ever larger, we trust that this volume will contain in its pages numerous beneficial ideas for those who have any occasion to profit from such information, whether it be from the standpoint of sporting pleasure, that of the hobbyist, or for the essential needs of experienced commercial fishermen.

Acknowledgments

WE ARE SINCERELY GRATEFUL to our many fishermen friends and to Marine museums and other sources too numerous to mention for the generous aid we have received, either directly or indirectly, during the preparation of this book.

To the following companies and individuals who also kindly contributed much valuable material, we are deeply indebted and we wish to acknowledge their assistance with gratitude and thanks:

R. J. Ederer Co., Chicago, Ill., for co-operation in supplying valuable details on commercial fishing nets from their popular publication *Commercial Fishermen's Reference Book.*

Atlantic Fisherman, Goffstown, N. H., for permission to use a series of illustrations with explanatory details on the mending and repairing of fish nets.

Outdoor Life, New York, N. Y., for permission to reprint the text and drawing of a method to prevent an anchor from fouling.

Chief of Engineers, United States Army, War Department, Washington, D. C., for permission to use material on the repair of fish nets included in Technical Manuals T M 5-268 and F M 5-20 H.

United States Department of the Interior, Fish and Wildlife Service, Washington, D. C., for permission to reprint information contained in certain printed and processed publications of the Fish and Wildlife Service.

Frank E. Firth and Carl B. Carlson, Technologists, Division of Commercial Fisheries, Washington, D. C., for the use of an article entitled, "Preservation and Care of Fish Nets."

W. T. Conn, Technologist, United States Bureau of Fisheries, Fish and Wildlife Service, Washington, D. C., for the use of two articles entitled "Net Preservative Treatments" and "The Tanning or Barking of Nets."

Captain William Alford and Captain Louis Pardiac, for supplying valuable suggestions on general fishermen's knots.

Eleanor Ewing, for the excellent drawings and lettering included herein.

Don Selchow and Lester Krauss, for producing the exceptionally fine photographs.

RAOUL GRAUMONT

ELMER WENSTROM

Table of Contents

		PAGE
PREFACE		v
ACKNOWLEDGMENTS		ix
LIST OF ILLUSTRATIONS		xiii
I	ANGLER'S AND STILL FISHERMEN'S KNOTS	1
II	COMMERCIAL FISHERMEN'S KNOTS . .	31
III	FISHING TRAPS AND SEINES	133
IV	NETMAKING AND REPAIRING . . .	145
INDEX		199

List of Illustrations

PLATE	TITLE	PAGE
1.	Attaching Lines to Leaders	2
2.	Blood and Barrel Knot Bends	4
3.	Useful Fishhook Ties	6
4.	Fishhook Ties for Turned-down or Turned-up Eyes	8
5.	Attaching the Turtle Knot to Fishhooks and Eyed Flies	10
6.	Attaching Droppers and Making Up Fishhooks	12
7.	Wire Leaders and Swivel Attachments	14
8.	Angler's Loops	16
9.	Dropper Loops	18
10.	Making Leader Loops and Attaching Dropper Strands	20
11.	Swivel Attachments and Other Knots	22
12.	Dropper Fly Hitches	24
13.	Dropper Fly Hitches, etc.	26
14.	Dropper Fly Hitches and Tackle Whippings	28
15.	Angler's Ties and a Crab Net	29
16.	Hitches	32
17.	Hitches	36
18.	Line to Leader, Hook, Swivel and Spinner Attachments, etc.	38
19.	Hitches and Bends	40
20.	Net Line, Ossel Hitches, etc.	43
21.	Stopper Hitches and Turk's-heads	46
22.	Simple and Useful Knots	50
23.	Useful and Decorative Knots	51
24.	Useful Knots	54
25.	Bowlines	56
26.	Bends and Sheepshanks	58
27.	Bends	61
28.	Bends	63
29.	Bends and Other Knots	64

30. Line Connections and Fishhook Ties   .   .   .   66
31. Miscellaneous Fishhook Ties   .   .   .   68
32. Fishhook Ties 70
33. Fishhook and Other Ties   .   .   . 72
34. A Surface Trawl   74
35. Miscellaneous Ties 76
36. Gut Leader and Other Ties 78
37. End Rope Knots   80
38. End Rope Knots and Splices   .   .   . 84
39. Eye and Cut Splices   86
40. Short and Long Splices   .   .   . 90
41. Splices, Grommets and Whippings   .   . 92
42. Whippings and Seizings   .   .   . 98
43. Rope Coils and Gaskets   .   .   . 102
44. Rope Ladder Making   .   .   .   104
45. A Shrimp Net, Harpoon Lashings and Fender . 106
46. Rope Pointing, Flemish and Spindle Eyes   . 108
47. Miscellaneous Knotwork   .   .   . 110
48. Emergency Fishhook Ties, Whaling Irons, etc. . 112
49. General Knotwork   .   .   .   116
50. Boatswain's Chair and Lashings   .   . 120
51. Method of Securing Hawsers   .   . 122
52. A Stage Sling and Belaying Pin Ties   .   . 124
53. Fishing through the Ice, A Grapple, Spears, etc. . 128
54. Tunnel, Fyke and Gill Nets   .   .   134
55. A Trammel Net and Seines   .   .   136
56. Rules for Gill Nets, Mesh Measurements and
    Hanging Nets   138
57. Trap Nets   139
58. Trap Nets   140
59. Pound and Hoop Nets   .   .   . 142
60. Netting Shuttles or Needles   .   .   146
61. Weaving Meshes   .   .   .   148
62. Mesh Weaving (Continued)   .   . 149
63. Lengthening the Chain 150
64. Weaving Body of Net   .   .   . 153

65. Proceeding with the Weave 154
66. Weaving Continued and Trimming a Tear . . 156
67. Formation of a Meshing Knot 158
68. Net Repairing 159
69. Net Repairing (Continued) 160
70. Net Repairing (Continued) 162
71. Patching a Net 164
72. Making a Narrower or Wider Row of Meshes, etc. 166
73. Reducing and Increasing Meshes 167
74. Increasing Meshes and Lock Knots . . . 168
75. Fish and Landing Nets 170
76. Instructions on How to Make a Landing Net . 174
77. A Standard Landing Net 180

65. Fragments, with thick forges 151
66. .... Chemical and .... Features of Iron 151
67. Formation of a Mechanical 152
68. Net Sharpening 159
.... Net Abrasion of ....
69. .... Net Abrasion (Continued) 192
70. .... Vise ....
.... Testing a Network of .... New York 200
71. .... Polishing and .... Blades 191
72. .... Machines .... Root 188
73. Paving and 191
74. Test .... Effect on the .... Breaking Half 191
.... Standard Specification ....

CHAPTER I

Angler's and Still Fishermen's Knots

THIS chapter is exclusively devoted to all knots and ties which are of practical use to anglers and still fishermen or, in other words, fresh-water fishermen. Therefore, it embraces numerous variations of almost every form of tie along this line that is known to have any practical use for certain purposes. For this reason, there are many odd and rare examples numbered among the large assortment illustrated and described herein. Some of these knots are seldom used by the majority, but they still have special appeal to many fishermen who prefer to use unique methods which they consider the best adapted for their own individual requirements and convenience.

On the other hand, we have exerted every effort to include in the contents of this chapter practically all of the better known and widely used methods that in the main are applied to the average daily pursuits of fresh-water fishing needs by the great majority of fishermen. Therefore, there are many interesting and practical examples included in this section of knotwork that are far too numerous to mention in a short summary of this nature. However, suffice it to say, one will find among this diversified assortment such popular and useful items as attaching lines to leaders, blood and barrel knot bends, fishhook ties, dropper ties, making up fishhooks, wire leaders and swivel attachments, angler's loops, dropper fly hitches and tackle whippings.

The overall contents of this section of knot work should serve practically every requirement for fresh water fishing, insofar as the preparation and application of various ties are concerned.

Additional information will also be found in the following chapter on salt-water ties, which contains numerous examples that are equally useful in fresh water.

1

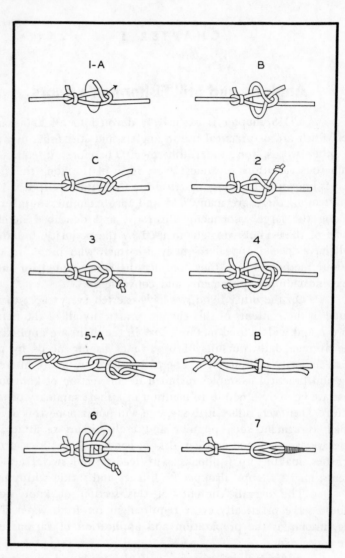

PLATE 1. Attaching lines to leaders.

Plate 1. ATTACHING LINES TO LEADERS

Fig. 1A—The SINGLE SHEET BEND TIE makes a reliable knot for connecting a line to a leader. It can be formed either in this manner, or in the opposite way to the example illustrated. The knot would then be reversed with the working end of the line leading down instead of up as it is here.

Fig. 1B—This illustrates the same tie after its formation has been completed.

Fig. 1C—It is shown here pulled taut against the leader.

Fig. 2—The SINGLE SHEET BEND TIE with overhand knot on the end of the line is often called a jam hitch by fishermen.

Fig. 3—The REEF KNOT or PINCH JAM, as it is sometimes called, makes a solid binding connection that will cinch up and hold fast under a strain. But when tension is released from the line this tie can be slacked off and undone without difficulty. It will be noted that an overhand knot is also used on the end of the line with this tie.

Fig. 4—The LORN or FIGURE-OF-EIGHT TIE at first appears to be rather complex, but in reality it is quite simple to duplicate, once its formation has been studied. It is one of the most popular forms of line to leader ties.

Fig. 5A—The OVERHAND or JAM KNOT TIE represents nothing more than the common overhand knot connection with the leader.

Fig. 5B—It is shown closed up in this illustration. If pulled up over the end of the leader loop, it is then transformed into a sheet bend when drawn taut. It will be noted that an overhand knot is used to form the leader loop here, whereas the angler's loop method is illustrated in the other examples. The difference in the formation of such loops is merely a matter of personal opinion. However, the angler's loop is recommended in preference to most other methods, as it has a more correct lead and will have less tendency to twist or distort the line.

Fig. 6—The TILLER or SLIPPED HITCH, in this case, is formed in the opposite manner to Plate 15, Fig. 83. Otherwise, there is no difference in the utility of its functions.

Fig. 7—The REEF KNOT or PERMANENT LOOP is preferred by many anglers on account of its convenience. The loop in the

3

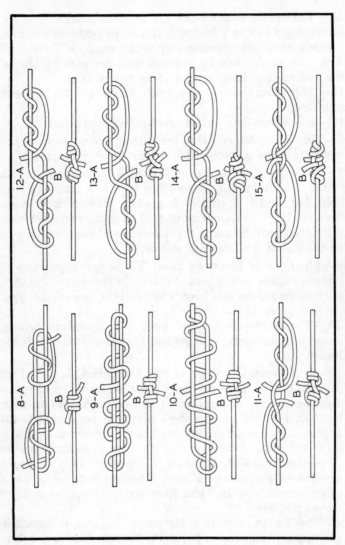

PLATE 2. Blood and barrel knot bends.

end of the line is seized, as indicated. It can be whipped through the water without causing any noticeable commotion.

Plate 2.   BLOOD AND BARREL KNOT BENDS

Fig. 8A—The DOUBLE FISHERMAN'S or BARREL KNOT BEND is one of the simplest and most uniform of more than a dozen variations of similar forms of ties that are used for uniting the ends of gut. There is very little difference in the effective utility of the knots on this plate and selecting a method to use is largely a matter of personal opinion, since these ties are all based on the same general principle of construction, with the difference in the pattern of the knot depending upon the number of turns taken with the gut on each half of the knot, and as to whether these turns are reversed or taken in an alternate direction to the opposite side.

Fig. 8B—This shows the compact appearance of the knot when pulled taut. These ties offer practically no resistance to the water.

Fig. 9A—The BARREL KNOT BEND shown here differs somewhat from the previous method. Its two turns are taken from the outside toward the center on each half of the knot, whereas in the former style the turns are taken from the inside toward the ends on each half of the knot.

Fig. 9B—The same knot completed.

Fig. 10A—Another BARREL KNOT BEND combination with open body to illustrate its method of construction.

Fig. 10B—As the finished product appears. This knot has a tendency to reverse itself while being pulled taut. This explains why the ends of the finished knot do not exactly correspond with the ends of the open illustration.

Fig. 11A—The BLOOD KNOT BEND shown here embraces a different style twist from the preceding method. However, it can be followed from the illustration much easier than words can describe its method of construction.

Fig. 11B—Same example drawn taut. Such knots as these are worked up with less difficulty if the slack is taken out gradually while carefully pulling the knot together.

Fig. 12A—The BLOOD KNOT BEND illustrated here represents an-

5

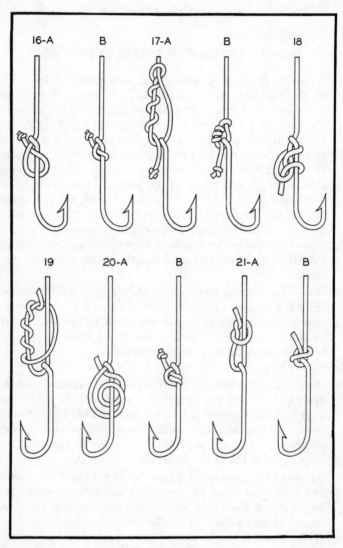

PLATE 3. Useful fishhook ties.

other method that is similar in construction to the previous example.

Fig. 12B—When finished the same knot will assume this appearance.

Fig. 13A—This BLOOD KNOT BEND differs very slightly from the last two shown.

Fig. 13B—This represents the finished tie.

Fig. 14A—The BLOOD KNOT BEND shown here is likewise similar to the previous styles of this tie.

Fig. 14B—This illustrates the knot closed.

Fig. 15A—This illustrates the final BLOOD KNOT BEND combination.

Fig. 15B—As the same tie will look when finished.

Plate 3.   USEFUL FISHHOOK TIES

Fig. 16A—The SINGLE SHEET BEND, or SINGLE BECKET HITCH, or JAM HITCH with overhand knot makes one of the simplest means of attaching a line to a hook.

Fig. 16B—After the slack has been taken out of the line, the knot will appear as shown here.

Fig. 17A—The TWIST KNOT FISHHOOK TIE is a rather clumsy knot when tied with large line, but when it is tied with small material, it cinches up into a rigid, compact tie.

Fig. 17B—It is shown here after being pulled partly taut.

Fig. 18—The INSIDE ROUND TURN FISHHOOK TIE will assume the shape of a blood knot if the top turn is worked down over the bottom turn as the knot is being pulled taut. It can then be worked up into a tie of perfect, symmetrical proportion that will be neat and serviceable.

Fig. 19—The TRIPLE TURN JAM KNOT is customarily used for gut substitutes.

Fig. 20A—The DOUBLE SHEET BEND, or DOUBLE BECKET HITCH, or DOUBLE JAM HITCH has two turns taken around the shank of the hook in similar manner to a sheet bend of this nature.

Fig. 20B—It is shown here as it appears when pulled taut. An additional overhand knot on the end of the line will add to the security of the tie.

Fig. 21A—The EYED FLY JAM or SLIDING OVERHAND KNOT repre-

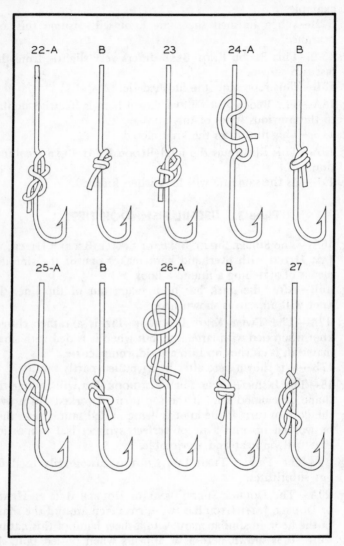

PLATE 4. Fishhook ties for turned-down or turned-up eyes.

sents a simple and effective manner of attaching gut to a fishhook.

Fig. 21B—It is illustrated here, after having been pulled up to the eye of the hook and adjusted. This knot should be cinched up hard and fast for effective and dependable use. It may either be pulled taut above the eye or below the eye of the hook.

Plate 4. FISHHOOK TIES FOR TURNED-DOWN OR TURNED-UP EYES

Fig. 22A—The CINCH or CONSTRICTOR KNOT FISHHOOK TIE offers an effective means of securing a line to a hook.

Fig. 22B—It is a reliable tie and cinches up snug and neat, as can be readily observed here.

Fig. 23—The FISHHOOK TIE shown here is somewhat different from the preceding method, but close study of its form of construction will show, "plainer than words can describe," how it is tied.

Fig. 24A—The WEDGE FISHHOOK TIE is a simple and popular method. The knot is slipped over the turned-down eye and comes to rest just below the bend after it is completed.

Fig. 24B—The finished job.

Fig. 25A—The WEMYSS EYED FLY KNOT or FIGURE-OF-EIGHT TIE is easy to form and in common use among fishermen.

Fig. 25B—Showing position the knot assumes after coming to rest below the turned-up eye of the hook.

Fig. 26A—The ROUND TURN or DOUBLE FIGURE-OF-EIGHT TIE is tied in practically the same manner as the previous method, except for the additional round turn.

Fig. 26B—The same tie as it appears when drawn taut below the eye of the hook.

Fig. 27—The RETURN, WOOD, SAFETY LINK, or SINGLE CAIRNTON KNOT is a modified form of the figure-of-eight tie. It is a favorite tie of many anglers, who prefer it for attaching their flies to leaders. Various names applied to the same knot may often be confusing. Names of many knots have little significance, because the same form of tie may be given a special name by men in different localities and in different professions.

9

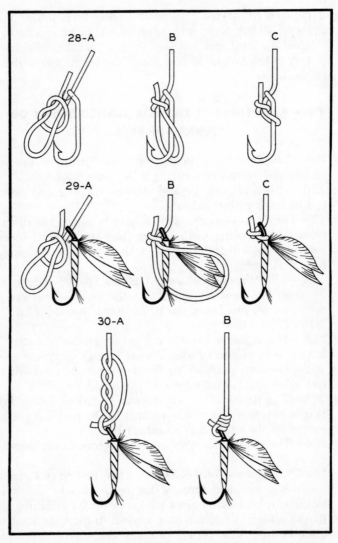

PLATE 5. Attaching the turtle knot to fishhooks and eyed flies.

Plate 5. ATTACHING THE TURTLE KNOT TO FISHHOOKS AND EYED FLIES

Fig. 28A—The TURTLE KNOT FISHHOOK TIE is shown here as it appears after the first step of forming a slip eye with an overhand knot has been completed.

Fig. 28B—The eye of the loop is next passed over and around the bend and shank of the hook, as it appears here.

Fig. 28C—To complete the tie, bring the loop up on the shank of the hook and let it come to rest just below the eye, as it is shown here. It is then pulled taut, thus making a secure and dependable fastening. This knot was first illustrated in an English fishing gazette many years ago, and since that time it has become the most widely known of all fishhook ties, as it undoubtedly represents the best method ever devised for attaching gut to hooks or eyed flies. It will hold equally well with gut or gut substitutes and with any kind of leader points.

Fig. 29A—Attaching the TURTLE KNOT to an eyed fly. The first stage of the operation is carried out in the same manner as in the preceding illustrations.

Fig. 29B—At this stage, take care to allow enough slack in the loop, so that the body and wings of the fly stay clear of any entanglement with the gut.

Fig. 29C—As the knot will appear after the line has been adjusted around the neck of the hook's eye. It is an equally effective tie with either turned-down or turned-up eyes.

Fig. 30A—A TWISTED KNOT such as this makes an excellent method for attaching an eyed fly to nylon.

Fig. 30B—As the completed knot appears when worked up into a symmetrical and neat shape.

Plate 6. ATTACHING DROPPERS AND MAKING UP FISHHOOKS

Fig. 31A—A SINGLE FISHERMAN'S KNOT, which consists of two overhand knots tied back to back, may be used to form a dropper attachment for a fly line with a knotted end.

Fig. 31B—When the knots are pulled together against the length of fly line, the tie will assume this appearance.

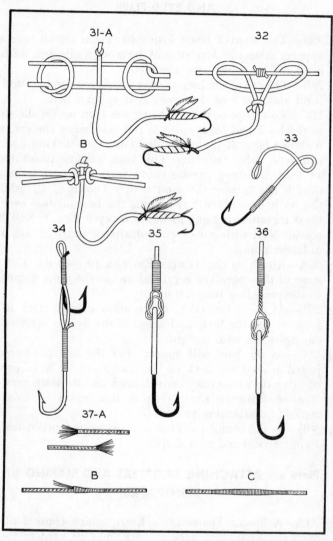

PLATE 6. Attaching droppers and making up fishhooks.

Fig. 32—A BARREL KNOT may also be used on the line, as illustrated, when attaching a fly by means of an angler's loop.

Fig. 33—A SNELLED HOOK such as this may have the gut seized in the following manner. When mounting tad or flattened hooks or any hook that has a taper, but has no eye or ring, lay a piece of waxed silk along the shank of the hook about halfway down, then continue by winding it back to the end of the shank. Next, a length of gut is tightly whipped along the shank around these turns and up to the bend of the hook to finish off. A coat of lacquer or varnish may then be applied if desirable. Large salt-water hooks will require heavier line for this purpose, such as seine twine or fishline. Fresh-water snells are usually made of gut, nylon, silk or horsehair. Hemp and flax have also been utilized for salt-water snells for many years. It is customary to thoroughly soak both gut and horsehair in warm water before tying knots with them.

Fig. 34—Various methods may be employed for making up hooks such as these, with the barbs turned or facing the same way or pointing in opposite directions. Whippings are used on the two lines, as illustrated, to unite the hooks.

Fig. 35—The MULTIPLE WIRE SEIZING is made up, as illustrated, with fine copper wire being used for the serving, which is soldered in a collar to finish off. Special tackle such as this is often necessary for barracuda or shark or any fish which have a habit of snapping at bait, thus increasing the possibility of cutting the line. Quite frequently hooks are mounted on chain for the same purpose.

Fig. 36—The MULTIPLE WIRE LONG SEIZING is twisted up as shown here and served with copper and soldered in the same manner as in the previous method.

Fig. 37A—A FISHLINE LONG SPLICE may be made by unraveling and fraying out the ends of a fishline, then taper the ends down by scraping them to a point.

Fig. 37B—Lay the ends parallel to each other, but facing in opposite directions, as shown in the previous illustration. Now start from the center and serve first one end and then the other with a tight whipping (Plate 14, Fig. 81). This shows only one end served.

13

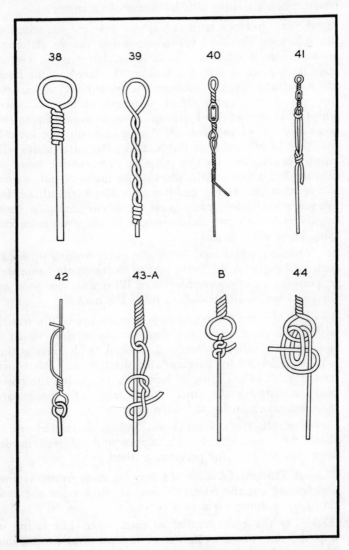

PLATE 7. Wire leaders and swivel attachments.

Fig. 37C—With both ends served, the splice is now complete. Apply a coat of lacquer to the finished job.

Plate 7. WIRE LEADERS AND SWIVEL ATTACHMENTS

Fig. 38A—ROUND EYE and SQUARE TWIST. A wire leader such as the one shown here is commonly used when fishing for certain kinds of salt-water fish that require strong leaders. Wire traces, similar to this method in construction are likewise required between lure and line for certain members of the pike family in fresh water. This prevents the fish's teeth from cutting the line. A leader of this type should be chosen for its strength and imperceptible manner of gliding through the water without attracting the attention of the fish. Plain, galvanized, high-carbon or stainless steel are used for most types of wire leaders. When plain wire is used it should never be trusted for more than one day's fishing, as it has a tendency to rust quickly and should be renewed often. Stainless steel is undoubtedly the best to use for general purposes, as it resists rust and if made up with care will give good service.

Fig. 39—A PIANO TWIST WIRE LEADER showing a different variation in the twist than that which was used in the previous method. This is one of the strongest single wire twists.

Fig. 40—A WIRE TO SWIVEL FASTENING may be employed, as shown here. Take care that while twisting the wires, both of them are twisted together, instead of one of them being twisted around the body of the other. This connection makes a good swivel attachment and, if applied properly, should not impede the functioning of the swivel.

Fig. 41—This shows how to ATTACH GUT TO A SWIVEL by means of a lark's head and overhand knot, which is a rather commonly used method, but not as practical as a number of other forms of ties that will follow.

Fig. 42—The SAFETY PIN and LOOSE HOOK connection is often used for cut baits.

Fig. 43A—This is a reliable method for attaching gut to a swivel and it is very simple to tie as can be readily observed.

Fig. 43B—Shows the same tie pulled taut.

15

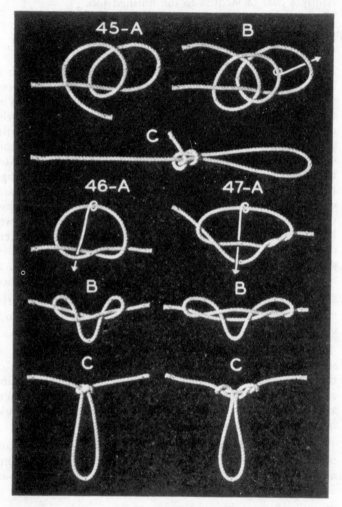

45-A   B

C

46-A   47-A

B   B

C   C

PLATE 8. Angler's loops.

Fig. 44—Another method for attaching gut to a swivel that pulls up into a neat, compact tie and holds fast.

Plate 8.   ANGLER'S LOOPS

Fig. 45A—The ANGLER'S LOOP is undoubtedly the most popular of all leader loops, as it is universally used by fishermen throughout the world. This method of looping the end of a leader, gut snells, etc., is not only easy to tie but also has a perfect lead which gives it a very uniform and compact appearance. It is begun by taking a turn around the standing part with the working end of the line, as illustrated.

Fig. 45B—The line is now brought under the first turn in the manner shown here. The first turn is then pulled through the loop, as indicated by the drawn-in line.

Fig. 45C—After the knot has been drawn taut it will assume this appearance.

Fig. 46A—The OVERHAND or THUMB KNOT LOOP is one of the simplest methods used for attaching a dropper fly. An overhand knot is formed and opened up in the manner shown. The body of the line is then pulled through the opening, as indicated.

Fig. 46B—This is how it appears with the loop partly pulled through the opening before being drawn taut.

Fig. 46C—The same knot after it is worked up snug and compact.

Fig. 47A—The HARNESS LOOP, sometimes called double harness loop, represents a sturdier method than the previous example but will require more line to tie. This shows how the tie is formed with an overhand knot with the end of the line being pulled out and then run back through the opening. The loop is then pulled through, as indicated.

Fig. 47B—With the loop pulled part way through before drawing taut.

Fig. 47C—The completed knot after working the slack out and pulling the loop down.

Plate 9.   DROPPER LOOPS

Fig. 48A—The LINEMAN'S LOOP or LINEMAN'S KNOT makes an excellent dropper loop, as it is simple and easy to tie and

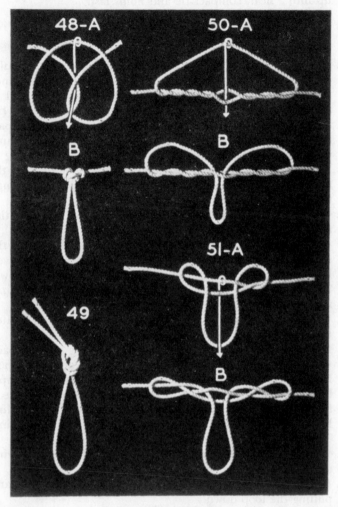

PLATE 9. Dropper loops.

serves the purpose well. Mountain climbers call this a butterfly knot. It is used by the middle man on the line of a three-man climbing team. This illustrates the preliminary stages of the knot with the drawn-in line showing how the loop is pulled through.

Fig. 48B—As the same knot will appear when drawn taut.

Fig. 49—The OVERHAND LOOP KNOT is often used as a dropper loop, but is not recommended as it does not have a proper lead and is not as strong as other more practical forms of this tie.

Fig. 50A—The MULTIPLE OVERHAND KNOT LOOP has four turns taken in the form of an overhand knot to complete the tie, which makes a practical dropper loop but is rather bulky and requires plenty of line to tie. This illustration shows how the loop is passed through the center of the twisted knot.

Fig. 50B—With the loop pulled part way through, it will then assume this appearance.

Fig. 51A—The DOUBLE HARNESS LOOP or Hitch, as it is often called, is begun by first tying the single harness loop, which is also called artillery loop or manharness knot (Plate 10, Figs. 52A and B). The drawn-in line now shows how the tie is completed.

Fig. 51B—The completed tie. It makes a useful dropper loop. Dropper loops should always be uniformly distributed along the length of the leader. In a case where two fly leaders are used, the dropper loop should be attached midway between the tail end of the leader and the line. When three flies are used, the dropper loops should be spaced three feet apart.

Plate 10. MAKING LEADER LOOPS AND ATTACHING DROPPER STRANDS

Fig. 52A—The MANHARNESS KNOT or ARTILLERY LOOP is known mainly for its utility as a means of hauling field guns into position with man power. However, it is probably one of the oldest forms of dropper loops used by anglers. This shows how the knot is begun, with the drawn-in line indicating the procedure used in completing the tie.

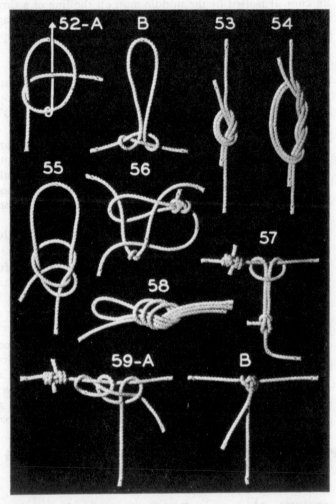

PLATE 10. Making leader loops and attaching dropper strands.

Fig. 52B—As it appears when finished.

Fig. 53—The SINGLE WATER KNOT, also called single surgeon's knot, is among the most reliable of line connection or leader-making knots. It is of simple construction and draws up snug and neat. It is used mainly as a means of attaching leader points.

Fig. 54—The DOUBLE WATER KNOT or DOUBLE SURGEON'S KNOT represents a somewhat more bulky tie than the previous method.

Fig. 55—The LEADER LOOP or PERFECTION LOOP, also called compound knot, represents the opposite or reverse way of tying the angler's loop (Plate 8, Fig. 45). It is likewise used as a leader loop or for a dropper point.

Fig. 56—Illustrates a method of ATTACHING A SNELLED FLY to a leader. It is sometimes called a dropper fly hitch. An angler's loop is tied around an overhand knot in this manner for security, while attaching the end of a dropper fly snell to a leader.

Fig. 57—Shows how to attach a LEADER LOOP.

Fig. 58—The LINE or LEADER LOOP shown here illustrates a slightly more complex manner of forming a dropper loop than Plate 9, Fig. 49.

Fg. 59A—Represents a method of attaching a DROPPER STRAND in a leader to line connection.

Fig. 59B—As the same tie appears when pulled taut.

Plate 11. SWIVEL ATTACHMENTS AND OTHER KNOTS

Fig. 60—A SWIVEL ATTACHMENT such as this serves equally well for spinners, ringed hooks, etc.

Fig. 61—The FIGURE-OF-EIGHT line to leader connection makes a dependable method that is easy to unite. In this case, the top part represents the leader and the bottom part is the line.

Fig. 62—The ADJUSTABLE LEADER LOOP needs no explanation, as it represents a well-known method that is easy to tie.

Fig. 63—A LEADER LOOP such as this may be slipped to prevent jamming. It is cast adrift instantly by jerking the end of the line.

21

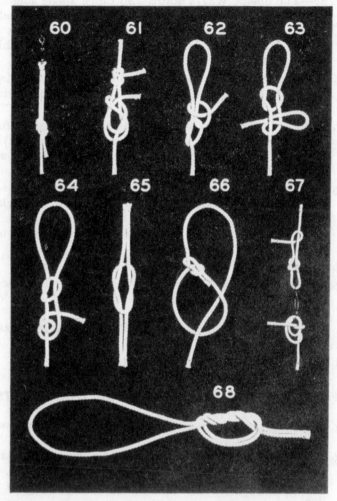

PLATE 11. Swivel attachments and other knots.

Fig. 64—A LEADER LOOP that is tied somewhat similarly, but in the reverse manner to a midshipman's hitch.

Fig. 65—The REEF KNOT BEND makes a good leader-to-line connection. It is a well-known tie that has been employed for various purposes since ancient times.

Fig. 66—A BOWLINE TIE such as this may be employed to form a slip loop.

Fig. 67—The SWIVEL HITCH is used on an angler's line. Quite often two swivels are also employed in the same manner, as illustrated here, to prevent jamming and thus give better service.

Fig. 68—The DOUBLED OVERHAND or GUT KNOT is employed in the end of a doubled snell, which is often used to add additional strength to and insure durable wearing qualities for a tie of this nature while serving its purpose. See Plate 30, Fig. 117, for the proper way to bend the end of a loop to the eye of a hook.

Plate 12. DROPPER FLY HITCHES

Fig. 69—The SINGLE WATER KNOT is sometimes utilized for attaching dropper flies, although it is not as popular as other methods with more appropriate leads.

Fig. 70—A BLOOD KNOT BEND that makes a good secure fastening for a dropper is shown here. An overhand knot is ordinarily used on the end of a dropper, as it is of simple construction and strong enough for general purposes.

Fig. 71—This form of tie has been in common use for many years as a means of attaching snells to leaders. It is similar to the example on Plate 10, Fig. 59.

Fig. 72—A DROPPER FLY HITCH that utilizes an overhand knot in the leader with the snell run through the overhand knot, as indicated. In this case, hooks are attached to both ends of the snell. If only one hook is used, the opposite end of the snell is knotted and hauled up snugly against the leader knot with the end cut short.

Fig. 73—A DROPPER FLY HITCH, such as that shown here, embraces a principle of construction similar to that of the weaver's knot, which is in reality a sheet bend, although it is tied in a slightly different manner. Double snells, such

23

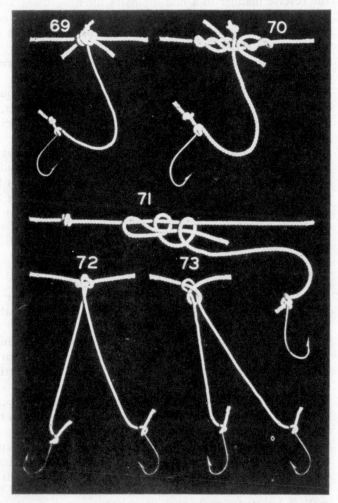

PLATE 12. Dropper fly hitches.

as this represents, are quite often clove-hitched to the end of a leader for salt-water fishing. In this case, an overhand knot is tied on the end of the leader below the clove hitch for security.

Plate 13. DROPPER FLY HITCHES, ETC.

Fig. 74—Shows an adjustable method that is particularly convenient for attaching droppers to leaders. Fig. *a* represents the dropper while Fig. *b* indicates the leader head.

Fig. 75A—The BLOOD KNOT or DOUBLE OVERHAND KNOT is one of the simplest and most practical of many similar forms that are numbered among the wide variety of barrel and blood knot bends which are used as stoppers on leader lines. This is necessary to keep dropper fly hitches from sliding along the leader line, thus holding them in their proper places.

Fig. 75B—As the same tie appears when drawn up.

Fig. 76—Another suitable method that holds the dropper almost at right angles to the leader.

Fig. 77—A DROPPER FLY or SNELL HITCH that comes from Captain Louis Pardiac of Bordeaux, France. This has been one of his favorite and most satisfactory methods for attaching droppers for a number of years.

Plate 14. DROPPER FLY HITCHES AND TACKLE WHIPPINGS

Fig. 78A—This DROPPER FLY HITCH automatically assumes the form of a sheet bend in the short end of a rope when the noose is pulled taut against the dropper.

Fig. 78B—After the transformation of this knot has taken place, while in the process of drawing it up, it will then appear as shown here.

Fig. 79—A simple method by which a swivel, spinner or ringed hook may be attached.

Fig. 80—A FOUR-STRAND BRAID such as this may be used to plait the shank of a hook with tarred fishline when anything more durable is not available, where special tackle is required for fish that are likely to sever the line by biting or snapping at baited hooks. Place the hook in a vise to hold it

25

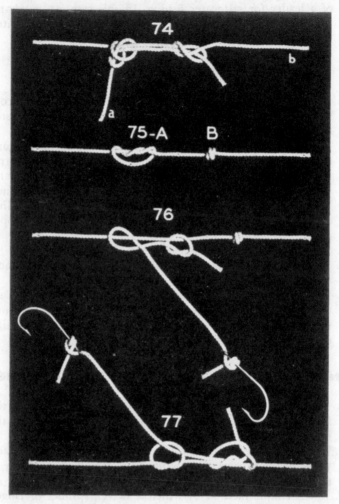

PLATE 13. Dropper fly hitches, etc.

rigid, then start braiding the shank with the fishline as illustrated. Strand *d* goes around, under the shank, and up between strands *a* and *b*, then over to its own side again. Strand *a* is next led under the shank, then up between strands *c* and *d*. To avoid confusion at this point, bear in mind that strand *d* is now lying below strand *c*, after the first pass was made with it, as previously described. Continue this same sequence until the braiding is finished and then finish off by splicing the ends into the tarred fishline in the same manner as an ordinary eye splice. See Plate 39, Fig. 170.

Fig. 81—TACKLE WHIPPINGS, which are often referred to as invisible knots by fishermen, are used to wrap or wind a rod. This illustration shows one of the commonest forms of starting and finishing this type of whipping.

Fig. 82—Another TACKLE WHIPPING that is a well-known and popular method. Both this and the previous methods are self-explanatory and need no elaboration. After whippings such as these are finished, cut the ends short, then give the material a light singe with an alcohol flame to produce a smooth job devoid of fuzzy particles.

Plate 15.   ANGLER'S TIES AND A CRAB NET

Fig. 83—A fisherman's method of attaching a line to a leader with a slip knot, which is an easy and effective way to unite such lines. It can be released without difficulty. This form of tie is also called a helm knot and tiller bend.

Fig. 84—A net such as this will be found useful for handling crabs. It is made similar to a landing net; but from 24- to 36-thread medium-laid seine twine is ordinarily used for this type of net instead of the smaller 18-thread line that is commonly used for other types of fish nets.

Fig. 85—An angler's method of attaching a line to a leader with a figure-of-eight tie.

Fig. 86—An angler's method of attaching a line to a leader with a single sheet bend or single becket hitch.

Fig. 87—An angler's method of attaching a line to a leader with a double sheet bend or double becket hitch. This tie is formed in the opposite manner to the previous method.

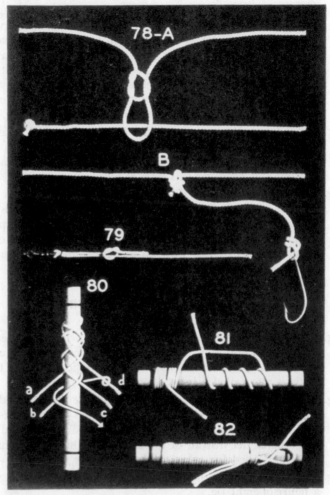

PLATE 14. Dropper fly hitches and tackle whippings.

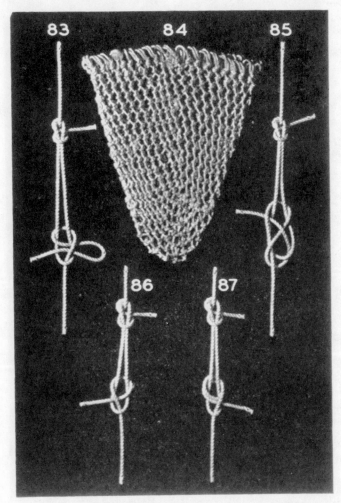

PLATE 15. Angler's ties and a crab net.

CHAPTER II

Commercial Fishermen's Knots

COMMERCIAL fishermen's knots, taken as a whole, are subject to rather broad interpretation, since they may cover not only the usual extensive variety of ties connected with fishing requirements, but also numerous sailor's knots that are used aboard trawlers, sperm whalers, etc., as a necessary part of the duties that are essential to the operation of all seagoing vessels, whether they be of the steamship or sailing ship variety.

With the requirements of this necessity in mind, we have undertaken to provide in this salt-water section of the book a most thorough selection of fishermen's knots and, on the other hand, a general variety of knots that may be applied to the usual duties of a sailor aboard ship.

It is therefore obviously assumed that an extensive work of this nature should include practically everything of interest or utility which a subject of this kind embraces.

The material contained here may be summarized as follows: Hitches of every kind with bends and Turk's heads, as well as simple and useful knots which are all included. Decorative knots are also dealt with, since this type of artistic-looking work is not only intended as a fitting tribute to the remarkable quality of fancy marlinespike seamanship that flourished among the sperm whalermen of the last century, but also as a stimulating reminder that this once great pastime which was the pride and joy of the oldtimers is not a forgotten art. On the contrary, much of their work is still preserved and anyone who finds beautiful designs of this nature to be of fascinating interest will acquire a surprising knowledge of the many additional examples by consulting *The Encyclopedia of Knots and Fancy Rope Work*.

Numbered among a host of other knots, there are many examples of outstanding usefulness listed here. Included are line connections and fishhook ties, surface trawls, gut leader and end

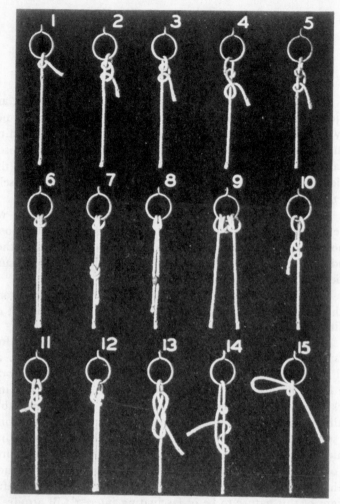

PLATE 16. Hitches.

rope knots. Splicings, whippings and seizings are also covered thoroughly. Rope coils and gaskets, rope ladder making, rope pointing, harpoon lashings, emergency fishhook ties, whaling irons, a boatswain's chair and lashings and methods of securing hawsers are likewise amply illustrated and explained. A stage sling and belaying pin ties, together with additional information on how to fish through the ice, concludes this part of the work.

The previous chapter containing fresh-water ties also has many examples of equal usefulness to salt-water fishing.

Plate 16. HITCHES

Fig. 1—The SINGLE HALF HITCH is the simplest hitch there is and forms the foundation for many important knots. It is very seldom used alone, except when the end is seized to the standing part.

Fig. 2—Two HALF HITCHES serve a variety of purposes, such as securing the end of a rope to a ring, spar or any other object. Their construction can be easily followed by observing the illustration.

Fig. 3—The SAILOR'S HITCHES shown here are tied in the reverse manner to the previous method. Hitches such as these are useful as mooring ties for small boats.

Fig. 4—The CLOVE HITCH on the standing part is used in the Navy to tie neckerchiefs. Its formation is easy to follow.

Fig. 5—The REVERSE CLOVE HITCH on the standing part is tied in the opposite manner to the previous method. This form of tie has very few uses.

Fig. 6—The LARK'S HEAD or COW HITCH is serviceable when an equal tension is applied on both standing parts, but is valueless when a strain comes on one part only. It is used on baggage tags or whenever a parcel is bound with the bight of a line. It can be tied in the middle of a line when the ends are inaccessible by passing a bight through the ring and flipping it back over the ring onto the standing part.

Fig. 7—The LARK'S HEAD STOPPERED shows an overhand knot used as a stopper for the lark's head. Knots such as this may be used to advantage when securing the end of a line to an anchor ring or any other similar object.

Fig. 8—The CROSSED LARK'S HEAD has the ends of the line coming out on opposite sides, as the picture illustrates, instead of through the bight as in the two previous methods. It is shown stoppered with a seizing.

Fig. 9—The TREBLE LARK'S HEAD is tied by forming a reverse bight with the ends passed through from underneath. A half hitch is then formed on each side, in the manner indicated.

Fig. 10—The BACKHANDED SAILOR'S HITCHES, first method, form another of the various ways of attaching a line to a ring. They are made by passing an end of the line around the inside of a ring, then under its own standing part and back around the ring again, and are finished off with two half hitches around the standing part.

Fig. 11—The BACKHANDED SAILOR'S HITCHES, second method, are tied in practically the same manner as in the previous method, except that the bottom hitch is tied in reverse, or in the opposite way from the first style of construction.

Fig. 12—The DOUBLE LARK'S HEAD shown here is begun by first tying the sailor's hitches illustrated in Fig. 3. Continue by doubling the top part back around the ring and then follow the standing part down through the hitch, which will complete the double form of this tie, as illustrated.

Fig. 13—The CAPSTAN KNOT is a variation of the figure-of-eight knot. It is used mainly as a temporary fastening, but is otherwise unreliable. Its construction can be easily followed from the illustration.

Fig. 14—The MIDSHIPMAN'S HITCH is more commonly known to yachtsmen and fishermen as a topsail sheet bend, acquiring its name from the use to which it is put. It consists of a half hitch made with the end around the standing part, plus a round turn inside half hitch just below it. This form of tie will not shake free when the strain on it is relaxed, hence its use for securing the end of the topsail sheet to the clew cringle in the sail. It is also used by tree climbers as a form of safety tie on their taut lines to adjust the proper height of their swing boards.

Fig. 15—The SLIP HITCH is made by first passing the line a full turn around the object to which it is to be attached. Then a full turn is taken around the standing part, and the bight of the end is tucked through the knot, in the manner illustrated. It may be used as a temporary fastening where it is necessary to untie the end of a line quickly, but it is not safe under a continued strain.

Plate 17. HITCHES

Fig. 16—The ANCHOR BEND, which is also known as a fisherman's bend, is a remarkable knot because of its simplicity and great strength. It will not slip, chafe, or jam. After withstanding severe tension, it can easily be untied when the strain on the line is eased.

Fig. 17—This shows an ANCHOR BEND tied in the opposite way to the previous manner and with a seizing attached, which is customarily employed for security when an additional half hitch is not used with this form of tie. Even then, a seizing is frequently applied to keep the knot from coming adrift.

Fig. 18—The FISHERMAN's BEND shown here follows the orthodox method of construction frequently used on yachts. The bend is formed in the following manner. First, take two round turns around the object to which it is to be attached. Then pass the working end around and under the standing part and through the round turn, forming a half hitch. Follow with another half hitch to make it secure. If the tension is not continuous it is better to seize the end to the standing part, since the knot is likely to shake itself free if the end is not secured. Fishermen often use this knot as a means of attachment for a chain cable. which is half chain and half rope.

Fig. 19—The RING HITCH is of simple construction and can be followed easily from the illustration.

Fig. 20—The BUOY HITCH can be used for any purpose that requires a safe, temporary tie that can instantly be undone by pulling on the end of the line forming the slip eye, after the line has been eased. Its method of construction can easily be followed from the illustration.

Fig. 21—The DOUBLE ANCHOR BEND is constructed in the same identical way as Fig. 16, but with its bottom part doubled to form a more compact tie of this nature.

Fig. 22—The LOBSTER BUOY HITCH is of quite simple construc-

35

transcient. It may be used as a temporary fastening where it is not necessary to make the end of a line quickly thimble is not ...

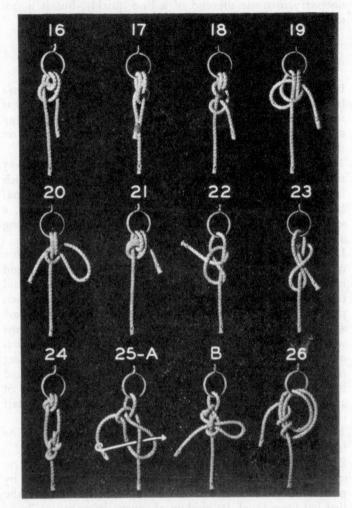

PLATE 17. Hitches.

line has been raised, the ... operation can easily be followed from the illustration ...

Fig 24—The Inside Anchor Bend is compared to the ... identically 26 Fig. 16, but with its bottom part unlimbered to form a more complex tie of different ...

Fig 25—This Inside ... but here it is quite simple and ...

tion and needs no explanation. In reality, it is nothing more than a lark's head tied on the standing part of the line. It holds well and will serve a variety of purposes.

Fig. 23—The BUNTLINE HITCH or STUDDING-SAIL TACK BEND is made by taking an inside clove hitch around the standing part. This hitch will jam hard and does not slacken. It is used to make fast the tack of the studding sail.

Fig. 24—The ANCHOR BEND AND BOWLINE makes an effective anchor bend tie for small boats. First form an anchor bend (Fig. 16), then a bowline is tied in the bottom part, as illustrated.

Fig. 25A—The MOGUL BEND or SAMPAN HITCH can be formed either as it is shown here or in the opposite or reverse manner, as is the case with most other types of knots. It is begun by forming a hitch around a bight, as illustrated. The working end of the line is next passed under the standing part and across the top of the bight to form another bight in the manner of a slip eye.

Fig. 25B—This shows the completed operation. It is used to moor skiffs and to lower such objects as small tools, so that the line can be drawn up again. It is also a popular tie in the Orient, where it is employed for tying up river craft of various kinds.

Fig. 26—A ROLLING ANCHOR BEND, such as this, represents an old English version of the present-day anchor bend.

Plate 18.   LINE TO LEADER, HOOK, SWIVEL AND SPINNER ATTACHMENTS, ETC.

Fig. 27—The FISHERMAN'S HITCH is basically the same as the anchor bend (Plate 17, Fig. 16), except for the slight variation in its method of construction, which can easily be observed by comparison. It is used primarily in making large hawsers fast.

Fig. 28—The LINE TO SWIVEL TIE shown here has its end seized to the standing part, after a round turn and a series of hitches have been made, as illustrated.

Fig. 29A—A LINE TO SWIVEL TIE, such as that shown here, is a durable and dependable method to use. Its construction is self-evident from the open illustration.

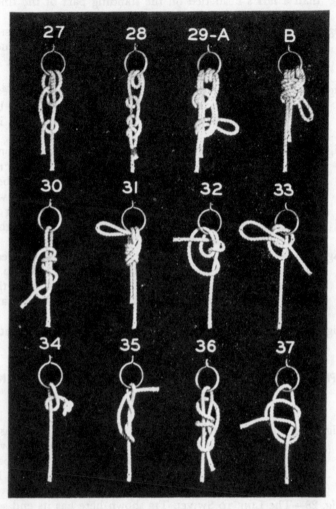

PLATE 18. Line to leader, hook, swivel and spinner attachments, etc.

Fig. 29B—As the same tie appears when drawn taut.

Fig. 30—The LINE TO SWIVEL TIE in this illustration is used mainly as a heavy-duty attachment.

Fig. 31—Another LINE TO SWIVEL TIE that makes a compact knot when worked up snug. It can be duplicated easily by following the illustration.

Fig. 32—This LINE TO SWIVEL TIE has a double turn taken through the eye of the swivel which gives a most secure and compact knot, when the gut is worked up gradually in a neat uniform body. When fastenings of this type are employed, care should be taken that the tie does not impede the operation of the swivel.

Fig. 33—The TEMPORARY FASTENING may be employed when a tie is required that can be quickly undone and cast off. It is instantly released by jerking on the end of the line.

Fig. 34—A SIMPLE TIE like this is useful for tying to ringed eye hooks and spinners.

Fig. 35—This form of tie can likewise be used on ringed eye hooks and spinners.

Fig. 36—Represents a NONFRICTION KNOT that will hold fast without slipping, when pulled taut. Exceptional care should be taken when tying synthetic line, such as nylon or Vec, to hooks, swivels, spinners, snaps or bait, as they do not contain the durable fibers of silkworm gut and, consequently, when improperly tied, may slip or wear through when subjected to an uneven strain.

Fig. 37—The LINE CONNECTION TIE shown here is a reliable method to use for uniting a line to whatever object it is to be attached. It is similar to the angler's loop (Plate 8, Fig. 45).

Plate 19.   HITCHES AND BENDS

Fig. 38—The CLOVE HITCH or RATLINE HITCH, which has a number of uses, is frequently employed to secure a line to a stanchion or spar, or to fasten the ratlines to the shrouds, hence its name. This very useful knot is not only easily tied, but is also quite secure when made on a spar. Its method of construction is quite easy to follow and needs no elaboration.

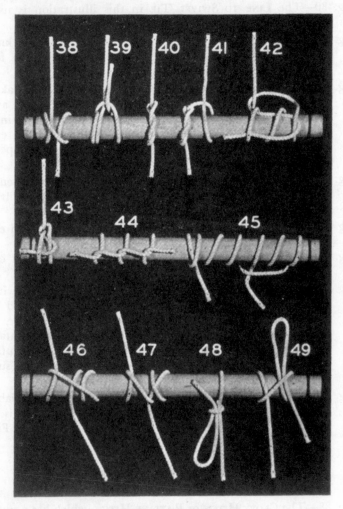

PLATE 19. Hitches and bends.

Fig. 39—The MAGNUS HITCH resembles the inside rolling hitch, but differs in that it has one overlapping turn which goes from the left side completely across the knot to the right side. It is formed by first making a round turn on the spar, then crossing over the two top turns and going completely around the spar again. The end is disposed of by putting it under the outside turn. This brings both ends of the line—or the working part and the standing part—out on opposite sides of the cross turn on top.

Fig. 40—The TIMBER HITCH is useful in securing a rope temporarily and quickly to a spar or piece of timber. It does not hold well unless it is kept taut. The twist should be in the same direction as the lay of the rope, which may easily be remembered by thinking of it as "dogged" with the lay.

Fig. 41—The KILLICK or KELLIG HITCH is an adaptation of the timber hitch with an additional twist taken with the working end of the rope, after a half hitch has been taken with the standing part around the object to which it is to be attached. It is a good way to secure a large stone or other object when a temporary anchor is needed. It is also used for certain lifting purposes. Fishermen often use it for anchoring seines, crab, eel and lobster pots.

Fig. 42—The TOPSAIL HALYARD BEND in this illustration is tied in the orthodox manner. This method is never used on merchant ships, but is sometimes employed on yachts. It is formed by first taking three round turns around a spar; next, the working end is brought back around the standing part and passed back under all three turns, then back over the last two and under the first turn again.

Fig. 43—The STUDDING-SAIL BOOM HITCH or STUNSAIL HALYARD BEND is made by taking a round turn around the spar. Then the end is brought around the standing part and back under the round turn and its own part. It is then tucked over the first part and under the second part in the opposite direction, as illustrated. This knot was used on the studding-sail booms of sailing vessels. It can also be formed by making the round turn on the opposite side of the standing part, with the working part of the line tucked from left to right to finish the knot.

41

Fig. 44—The MARLINE or HAMMOCK HITCH consists of a number of overhand or thumb knots (as many as necessary) made consecutively around an object, such as a yard, boom, stanchion. It has many uses, such as "marling down" the nettles or foxes when pointing a rope. Sails, bundles, or packages may be kept in a neat roll by marling them down with light rope. The marline is also a very useful hitch to apply when setting up wind dodgers to the jackstays.

Fig. 45—A REEF PENNANT HITCH is used to secure the reef cringle to the boom. A reef pennant is a rope that passes through a comb cleat on the end of the boom, through the reef cringle on the sail, then down through a comb cleat on the opposite side of the boom.

Fig. 46—The INSIDE ROLLING HITCH is tied as follows: Take a turn around the spar and then bring the line over the standing part and cross it to the opposite side of the spar. Continue by taking a round turn on the inside of the cross turn which will bring the working part out on the inside of the knot. This is the correct way the turns should be taken in bending a line to a spar. This is a valuable knot ashore or afloat, because it can be tied around a smooth surface without slipping. It can also be untied very easily. Another important feature of this knot is that it may be applied either at a right angle to the spar or parallel with it.

Fig. 47—The ORTHODOX ROLLING HITCH, sometimes called outside rolling hitch, is tied by taking a turn around the spar, then bringing the line to the opposite side of the spar and making two turns, bringing the line back under both parts, as illustrated. This is the method that is employed to bend a line to a rope.

Fig. 48—The SLIP HALTER HITCH is formed by putting the end of the line about the object or spar to which it is to be fastened, and then tying an overhand knot around the standing part. The end is then tucked back through the body of the knot. This hitch can be easily untied by pulling the end.

Fig. 49—The SLIP CLOVE HITCH is a variation of the ordinary clove hitch. It is made in the same way except that on the last tuck the bight, rather than the end, is placed under the turn. This is a handy knot, as it can be slipped and untied quickly.

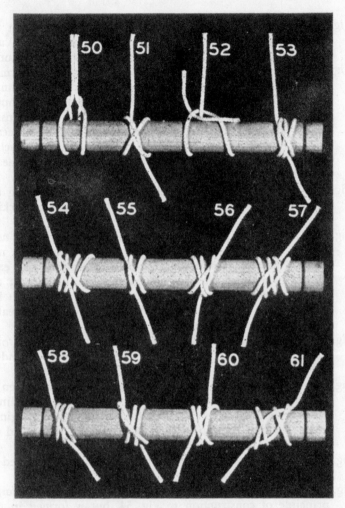

PLATE 20. Net line, ossel hitches, etc.

Plate 20. NET LINE, OSSEL HITCHES, ETC.

Fig. 50—The KELLIG or SLINGSTONE HITCH is in common use among fishermen as an anchor attachment for crab and lobster-pot gear, which are secured by means of heavy stones.

Fig. 51—The CINCH or CONSTRICTOR KNOT is a common form of tie that is easily converted from a clove hitch by the simple expedient of tucking one of the ends underneath the opposite part from the outside, which brings it out on the inside of the knot between the two cross turns. It is more secure than a clove hitch and binds hard and fast when well cinched up. It may be used to secure double gangings or as a means of fastening a fishline to a hook.

Fig. 52—An OSSEL HITCH such as this is used for attaching the ossels or short lengths of a net to the heavy rope or backing of the net.

Fig. 53—The OSSEL KNOT or NET LINE HITCH shown here is used on the head ropes, or small ropes along the top of a net. Head ropes are of opposite lay and run parallel with each other. Two ropes are used in this manner to prevent the entanglement and twisting of the net when wet, which has a tendency to roll up at the edges and become unmanageable when a single head rope is employed.

Fig. 54—Another NET LINE HITCH. It is similar to the last one, but with an additional cross turn and with the lower end of the line leading out in a slightly different manner.

Fig. 55—A GROUND LINE HITCH that is used by cod fishermen in attaching the ground line of their trawls to ganging lines. The method by which hooks are fastened to the gangings, after they are secured to the ground line, is illustrated on Plate 30, Fig. 117.

Fig. 56—This example of another NET LINE HITCH is formed in the opposite manner to Fig. 53.

Fig. 57—The NET LINE HITCH shown here employs a similar principle of construction to Fig. 54, but is formed in the opposite manner.

Fig. 58—A NET LINE HITCH which serves the same purpose as previous hitches of the same nature.

Fig. 59—Another NET LINE HITCH which illustrates a different formation of this type of knot.

Fig. 60—The final example of Net Line Hitches which is tied in the opposite manner to a ground line hitch with an additional round turn.

Fig. 61—An Eskimo Spear Lashing such as this is more decorative than practical. Most of the knots on this plate come from Captain William Alford, who fished the Grand Banks before the turn of the century.

Plate 21. STOPPER HITCHES AND TURK'S-HEADS

Fig. 62—The Stopper Hitch is formed by making a half hitch with the end of the line around the spar, rope, chain, or whatever it is to be used on. Then the end is backed around the object in the opposite direction from which the strain is to be applied. In use, the part hanging down should lead to the right, almost parallel to the object upon which it is fastened, and should be made fast to a stationary object. After the turns have been dogged around the rope or spar, the end is held in the hand. The authors have found that in actual practice these backing turns should always be taken with the lay of the rope (if it is put on a rope), as they tend to hold better, due to the added cross-friction. The regular stopper hitch shown in Fig. 64 is superior to this one, because the added turn gives it greater holding power, and if a heavy weight is to be suspended, it is much safer to use the stopper with more than one turn.

Fig. 63—The Two Half Hitch Stopper Hitch is used for the same purpose as the stopper hitch in Fig. 62, although made somewhat differently. Every person who uses a stopper knot has his own pet method of tying it. Some prefer the rolling hitch or one of the various other types. Experimentation has shown that, if applied to a rope, two half hitches are the most satisfactory, because the knot can still be cast free easily even when a great amount of tension is applied to it. The regular stopper hitch shown in Fig. 64 usually jams when a heavy weight is placed on it. Tension is applied to the knot in the direction indicated by the arrow.

Fig. 64—The Regular Stopper Hitch is the most widely used of all stoppers. This hitch will hold even when the rope is wet or greasy, because the heavier the load, the tighter the knot

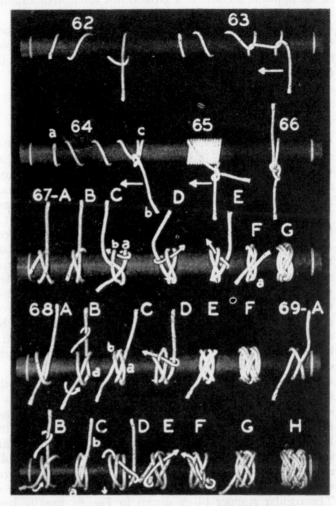

PLATE 21. Stopper hitches and turk's-heads.

becomes. In this case, as in all stoppers, the end made fast to the bitts or other object is marked *b,* and the end held in the hand is marked *a.* End *a* was left short in the illustration for obvious reasons, but in reality it is a little longer. First, take a turn around the rope, forming a half hitch. Next, take another turn around the rope and inside the original half hitch. The end should then be at point *c,* from where it is taken back and dogged with the lay. Notice the difference between this hitch and the hitch shown in Fig. 62. Tension is applied to the knot in the direction shown by the arrow.

Fig. 65—The LIFTING or WELL PIPE HITCH will also bear a strain parallel to the object to which it is fastened. It is used to secure the guy ropes of a circus tent to stakes driven into the ground or, as the name indicates, to hold a well pipe being lowered into the earth. It is formed by first taking a number of round turns about the object, as many as desired (the more the better). Then when enough have been put on, the end is brought across the top of the turns, and two half hitches are made around the standing part. Tension is applied to the knot in the direction shown by the arrow.

Fig. 66—The WEAVER'S HITCH is really a bowline, but is made like a weaver's knot or a sheet bend. This is a very useful method of hitching a line to a spar or other object, because it will not give and is easily untied.

Fig. 67A—THREE-STRAND TURK'S-HEAD, first stage, is represented in this illustration. Now turn your work to B.

Fig. 67B—This shows the second stage of the work, with the free end taken from the right, up and between the two turns.

Fig. 67C—The turn *a* is to be pulled under the turn *b,* as shown by the drawn line.

Fig. 67D—The knot will now look as shown here. The turn on the right-hand side was pushed to the left and under the left-hand turn. The moving end is now passed, as shown by the arrow.

Fig. 67E—This shows how the Turk's-head should look after the tuck has been placed as described in D. The moving part is now taken from the right to the left, under and up through the center, as the drawn line indicates.

Fig. 67F—The work is again turned, to position F. At this position, *a* indicates the movement just executed in E. The working end was on the right-hand side, and has been passed through the right to the left. The Turk's-head is now complete, and all that is necessary is to follow the standing end with the moving end. However, be sure to watch that the passes taken to double the Turk's-head do not cross each other. After following around twice, the Turk's-head appears as in G.

Fig. 67G—This shows the Turk's-head as it looks when finished, if the directions have been carefully followed. As a rule, three passes are made to complete most forms of Turk's-heads, however, only two passes are used here in order to clarify the illustrations.

Fig. 68A—FOUR-STRAND TURK'S-HEAD.

Fig. 68B—Notice that at *a* the moving part goes under both turns, instead of over and under.

Fig. 68C—The working end is then brought completely around the spar on the left-hand side, to the left of all the turns which have already been taken, and is brought over *b* and under *a*, which will lock these strands.

Fig. 68D—The work is again turned until position D is reached. (Some of the turns may slip out of place as the knot is being worked on, and should be adjusted until they resemble the illustration.) At this point, the working end is put over, under, and over as the drawn line indicates. This is the final tuck to be made in the Turk's-head and the work when turned appears as in E.

Fig. 68E—The moving end here follows the beginning, as in the three-strand Turk's-head, until two or three passes are made. The ends are then put underneath the Turk's-head before it is drawn up; after it has been worked tight around the spar, the ends are cut off close.

Fig. 68F—The FOUR-STRAND TURK'S-HEAD, when finished, appears as illustrated.

Fig. 69A—Beginning a FIVE-STRAND TURK'S-HEAD. The first two movements A and B are in this case the same as for the three-strand Turk's-head.

Fig. 69C—The end is brought completely around the spar on the left-hand side of the knot, to the left of all the turns, as in C of the four-strand Turk's-head just described. In this illustration, *a* is the standing part, and *b* is the moving part. The moving part is brought over and under, following strand *a,* to the right-hand side.

Fig. 69D—The work at this stage is turned to correspond with the illustration D, the drawn line indicating where the strand is to be put over, under, and over.

Fig. 69E—The work is now turned over, to correspond with E. At this point, the two parallel strands are split and the moving strand is passed, as the drawn line shows.

Fig. 69F—The work is again turned until this position is reached. The moving part is then passed between the parallel strands under, over, under, and over for the last tuck to complete the Turk's-head as shown in G.

Fig. 69G—The moving end at this point follows the original beginning until two or three passes have been made.

Fig. 69H—The Turk's-head is now complete and appears as in H. The ends are placed underneath and the work drawn taut. Turk's-heads have many uses, such as decorations for handrails, stanchions, etc.

Plate 22. SIMPLE AND USEFUL KNOTS

Fig. 70—Shows an Overhand or Thumb Knot. It is the most common form of tie in existence, being used by almost everyone for many different purposes. It is often used as a stopper knot to prevent a rope from running out of a block or falling through an opening. However, it should be used in this manner only as a temporary tie, because the knot has a tendency to jam hard under strain and is difficult to untie afterward. Furthermore, it should never be used in preference to the proper form of whipping or fraying. A rope with an overhand knot tied in its body should never be used without first untying the knot, as a rope with a knot in it possesses less than one-half the breaking strength of an unknotted rope.

Fig. 71A—The Figure-of-Eight Knot is often used as a stopper knot because it does not jam and opens quite easily. It has few uses as a practical knot, but is popular for ornamental work as it makes a very decorative tie and is simple in design.

Fig. 71B—The same knot as it appears when finished.

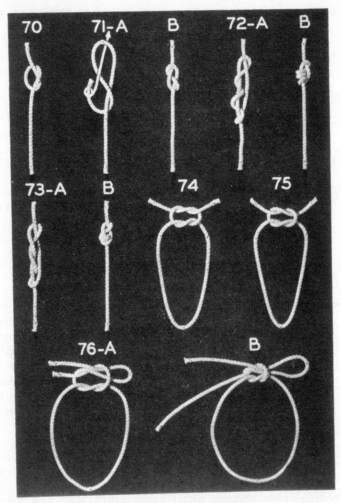

PLATE 22. Simple and useful knots.

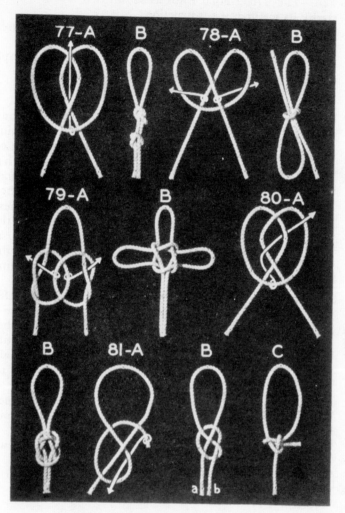

PLATE 23. Useful and decorative knots.

Fig. 72A—The THREE-FOLD KNOT is shown here opened up to clarify its method of construction.

Fig. 72B—This shows the same knot pulled taut. It can be used to weight the end of a line.

Fig. 73A—The STEVEDORE'S KNOT, opened up in this photograph to illustrate its method of construction, is used mainly to prevent the end of a rope from unreeving.

Fig. 73B—This shows the completed knot.

Fig. 74—The GRANNY KNOT is the most dangerous form of knot in existence, as it is often tied by mistake while attempting to tie the more secure square knot. It should never be used for any purpose, as it is completely untrustworthy and either slips or jams when subject to tension or strain. The beginner should study closely the characteristics of this knot and then compare it with the square knot that is shown in the next illustration. It will be noticed that the working ends of the line lead out in the opposite manner to the standing part after the knot is formed, whereas in the square knot the working ends lead out in the same manner as the standing part.

Fig. 75—The SQUARE or REEF KNOT is the oldest and most useful method of joining two pieces of cordage. It is used for a large variety of purposes, such as tying up bundles or other objects, or to tie the reef points in a sail. However, it should never be used if the ropes are of different sizes or materials, as it jams hard under tension. Do not join two hawsers together by this method. The reef knot is formed by tying an overhand knot first, then another overhand knot is formed in the opposite manner on top of the first one, as the picture illustrates.

Fig. 76A—The SQUARE or REEF KNOT with a bow is shown opened up in this illustration.

Fig. 76B—The same knot as it appears when pulled taut. It is used primarily as a shoelace tie.

Plate 23.   USEFUL AND DECORATIVE KNOTS

Fig. 77A—The SINGLE FISHERMAN'S KNOT is ordinarily used to tie gut, which is less likely to slip when tied with this form of knot than when joined with a reef knot or sheet bend. It is tied with the underhand loop on the left overlapping the underhand loop on the right, in the manner shown. The bight is then pulled through as the drawn-in line indicates.

Fig. 77B—The completed knot. This knot is often called an Englishman's, true lover's or waterman's knot.

Fig. 78A—The TOM FOOL'S KNOT or ARIZONA HANDCUFF HITCHES, also known as a conjurer's knot, is said to have been used as a rope handcuff in the early days of the West. It can also be used as a jar or pitcher sling. It is tied by forming a loop, in the manner shown, with one part of the line crossing over and the other part crossing under the knot. The bights are then pulled through, as indicated.

Fig. 78B—The completed knot is shown here.

Fig. 79A—The SHAMROCK KNOT is a simple ornamental knot of exceptional beauty, used extensively for decorative purposes. It is tied by forming two interlocking overhand knots with the ends in reverse to each other. The drawn-in lines show how each inside part is then pulled through the body of the two overhand knots to form the outside bights.

Fig. 79B—This represents the completed knot. This knot looks more attractive when doubled.

Fig. 80A—The INDIAN BRIDLE, THEODORE or HACKAMORE KNOT was first used as a decoration on the horsehair bridle of the early Indians. Later, it is said to have been used in the West as a temporary rope bridle and bit. There are several other names for this knot, such as jug sling; and in England it is known as a bag, bottle, or beggarman's knot. However, many of these names could also be applied to other knots; on the whole, the best choice seems to be Indian bridle or hackamore. The Indian bridle is tied by making two loops, with the inside part on the right overlapping the inside part on the left, as illustrated here. Next, pull the bottom bight up under the inside loop on the left, and between the overlapping center—going over, under, and over, as illustrated by arrow. Now invert the loops in front and back of the bight, and the knot appears as in Fig. 80B. By inserting the center of the knot over the neck and pulling taut, this knot may be used to close the end of a bag or to make a handle or sling to carry a bottle or jar. Fishermen use it for fastening bladderfloats to their nets.

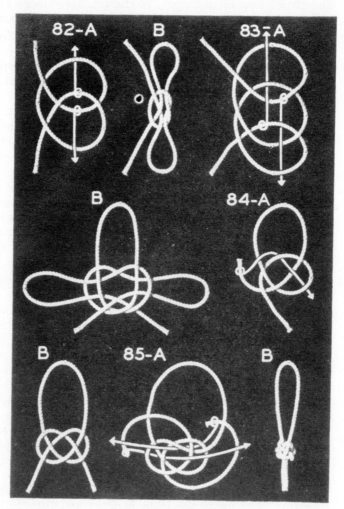

PLATE 24. Useful knots.

Fig. 81A—The CRABBER'S EYE KNOT is begun by laying the line out, as shown here, with the working part crossed under and then over the opposite part of the line. It is then run through the eye and passed underneath and out through its own part, as the drawn-in line indicates.

Fig. 81B—This shows the completed knot as described in Fig. 81, A. Before the knot is pulled taut it can be used as a running knot, as part *a* will function in the same manner as an ordinary slip knot. When part *b* is hauled upon, the knot jams in the form of a sheet bend, thereby making it a secure tie under strain.

Fig. 81C—The same knot as it appears when hauled taut.

Plate 24. USEFUL KNOTS

Fig. 82A—The SINGLE JURY MAST or SPANISH KNOT is begun by forming two loops with one overlapping the other in the manner shown, then the bights are pulled through, as the drawn-in lines indicate.

Fig. 82B—This shows the completed knot. Knots such as this are often used in the body of sheepshanks.

Fig. 83A—The DOUBLE JURY MAST KNOT is used for rigging a jury mast. The three bights form a means of attaching supports to the mast. The center of the knot is slipped over the masthead, and stays are bent to the three bights by using sheet bends. The ends are joined with a bowline, with one of the ends serving as a fourth stay, in order to complete the staying of the jury mast. The knot is formed by three overlapping loops. The loops are pulled through, as the drawn-in lines indicate, placing each bight on the opposite side. The center bight is pulled out on top.

Fig. 83B—Illustrates the completed knot as it appears when the bights have been pulled through to the outside.

Fig. 84A—The SAILOR'S BREASTPLATE shown here represents a double carrick bend tied in the end of a bight. It is made with an underhand loop crossed under, by reversing the strand pointing toward the right, as the picture illustrates, and then passing it underneath the body of the knot to the left side. It is then closed up with the strand from the left

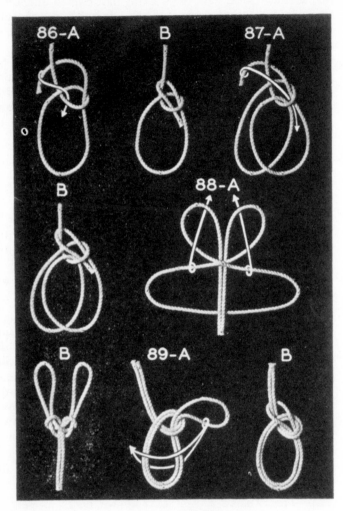

PLATE 25. Bowlines.

side, as indicated in the photograph by the drawn-in line.

Fig. 84B—The knot as shown here represents the completed operation. This knot is useless and is made mainly as an ornamental version of the double carrick bend.

Fig. 85A—The Two-Strand Carrick Diamond Knot is made by first forming a sailor's breastplate with one end of the line coming out on the inside of the loop and the other end coming out on the outside of the knot, as shown. Next pass both strands underneath and out through the middle of the knot, as illustrated by the drawn-in lines. Continue by pulling the knot taut while, at the same time, each strand is worked up and into place uniformly.

Fig. 85B—This shows the knot as it should look when pulled up properly. It is a very attractive and popular knot and is widely used for decorative purposes.

Plate 25. BOWLINES

Fig. 86A—The Bowline is sometimes called the king of knots, and is the most useful way to form a loop in the end of a rope. Though simple in construction, it never slips or jams; and after severe tension has been applied to it, a simple push of the finger will loosen it enough to untie. The bowline is really a sheet bend with a loop, but is made somewhat differently To make it, take the standing part in the left hand. The end, held in the right hand, is then laid on top of the standing part and grasped with the thumb and the index finger, the thumb being underneath. Next it is twisted up and away from you until Fig. 86A is reached. Then the end is put around the standing part and down again through the loop, as the line shows.

Fig. 86B—This represents the finished bowline.

Fig 87A—The French Bowline, or the Double Chaise de Calfat (double caulker's chair), is superior to the ordinary bowline as a sling, because it allows a man to use both hands. It is especially advisable to use this bowline when lowering a man into a smoke-filled hold or wherever there is danger of his losing consciousness, as it is impossible for a man to drop out of this type of sling. The formation of the French bowline is illustrated in its first stage in Fig. 87A.

57

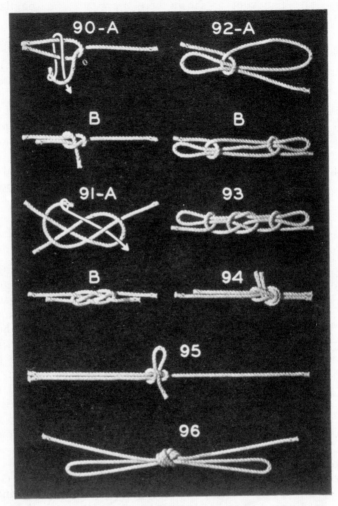

PLATE 26. Bends and sheepshanks.

Fig. 87B—This shows the finished French bowline as ordinarily used. A man sits in one of the loops, passing the other one about his chest and back under the armpits. The man's weight in one loop draws the other loop under the arms taut.

Fig. 88A—The SPANISH BOWLINE may be tied in many different ways. But this method is the simplest to illustrate. It is made with the bight of a rope, and laid out, as shown. The two bights on each side on top are then put through the loops on the bottom, as indicated by the drawn line.

Fig. 88B—This shows the Spanish bowline after the bights have been passed through the loops, and the knot drawn up tight. The knot pictured here can be used as a form of chair to sit in, although the French bowline is preferable for this purpose.

Fig. 89A—The BOWLINE ON THE BIGHT is formed on the bight of a line when the ends are inaccessible. To tie this knot, the bight of a rope is laid out to correspond with the illustration. It will be noted that the first step conforms to the beginning of the ordinary bowline. The drawn line indicates how the bight is passed around the bottom of the knot, then up again around the standing part. To the novice, this knot may seem quite mysterious and difficult, but it is really very simple to master. Many years ago, mischievous boys would tie this knot in the reins of a horse while the driver was engaged elsewhere. When he returned, he usually found it necessary to unhitch the reins from the horse's head in order to straighten them out and untie the knot.

Fig. 89B—This shows the finished bowline.

Plate 26. BENDS AND SHEEPSHANKS

Fig. 90A—The RIGHT-HANDED SHEET or BECKET BEND is also known as a single bend, common bend, simple bend and swab hitch. It was once in very common use as a means of bending a sheet to the clew of a sail. When the lines employed are of different sizes, always use the larger line for the bight or loop and the smaller to form the knot. It is made by forming a bight in one rope and a half hitch with the other rope, as the drawn line indicates. Weavers use this knot when a thread in a loom breaks. It has also been used for centuries in the making of nets.

59

Fig. 90B—Shows the finished sheet bend.

Fig. 91A—The DOUBLE CARRICK BEND has the line laid out, as shown, to form the pattern of the knot. The drawn line shows how the knot is closed up.

Fig. 91B—This shows the completed carrick bend.

Fig. 92A—The ORDINARY SHEEPSHANK is used for shortening a rope. The rope is first laid out to form two bights. A half hitch is then formed on each end of the bights, as shown on the left side of this illustration.

Fig. 92B—This shows the finished sheepshank.

Fig. 93—The MAN-O'-WAR SHEEPSHANK has a Spanish knot tied in the middle of the bights.

Fig. 94—The SHEET BEND ON A BIGHT is formed the same way as the regular sheet bend, but with two ends of the line instead of one. This knot is employed when two tackles are used.

Fig. 95—The SLIP SHEET BEND can be released instantly by pulling on the end of the slippery hitch.

Fig. 96—The OVERHAND SHORTENING is formed by tying an overhand knot in the middle of two bights, which have been made as though for a sheepshank.

Plate 27. BENDS

Fig. 97—A SINGLE RIVERMAN'S BEND, as shown here, is similar to a sheet bend, except that the first turn is taken on the outside instead of on the inside of the knot. It is very secure for a line that is slippery.

Fig. 98—A DOUBLE RIVERMAN'S BEND, the same as the single method except for an additional round turn.

Fig. 99—A RIVERMAN'S BEND with bow. It is easy to upset and cast off.

Fig. 100—The OVERHAND or GUT or LEADER BEND is formed by tying an overhand knot in one rope, then following the knot around with the other rope. This is used by fishermen to splice gut leaders. To soften it, the gut should always be moistened before tying.

Fig. 101A—The TRUE LOVER'S, ENGLISHMAN'S, FISHERMAN'S or HALIBUT BEND is also called water and waterman's knot, single waterman's loop, etc. It is made by tying two over-

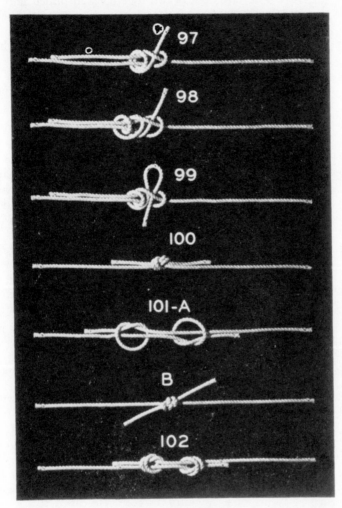

PLATE 27. Bends.

hand knots back to back around the standing part of opposite lines. They are then drawn together and pulled taut. It is a strong tie, will hold fast and is in common use among anglers.

Fig. 101B—It will appear neat and compact, as shown here, when pulled taut.

Fig. 102—The DOUBLE ENGLISH KNOT, DOUBLE WATER LOOP or GRAPEVINE KNOT is commonly employed by anglers for knotting silkworm gut and horsehair.

Plate 28.   BENDS

Fig. 103—The FISHERMAN'S KNOT, also called water knot and leader knot, is used for uniting the ends of gut. It is basically the same knot as Plate 27, Fig. 101, except that the two additional hitches are tied separately instead of interlacing with the overhand knots.

Fig. 104A—The BARREL or BLOOD KNOT BEND illustrated here represents another one of the many different versions of this tie. Bends such as this make excellent knots for any kind of small fishline that is slippery and hard to handle. With a snug, compact knot worked up properly, this knot offers little if any resistance to the water, and will always be dependable when subjected to a strain.

Fig. 104B—As the same tie appears when pulled taut.

Fig. 105—The GUT LEADER BEND shown here is made by tying a twisted hitch around the standing parts of both lines.

Fig. 106—Represents another BARREL or BLOOD KNOT BEND with three round turns on both sides of the knot. This gives it a sturdier-looking body than the two previous examples. However, the additional turns are unnecessary as they do not improve the function of this form of tie.

Fig. 107A—The RING, GUT or WATER KNOT BEND derives its name in part from the father of anglers, Izaak Walton, who died at Winchester, England, in 1683. He called it a water knot. However, in later times the same tie came to be known as a ring knot or gut knot. It is shown here opened up with the drawn-in lines indicating how the knot is completed. The finished version of this tie is shown on the following plate.

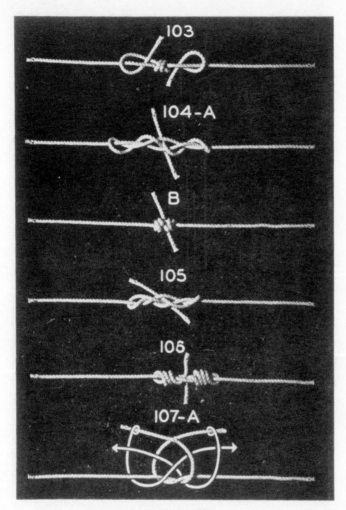

PLATE 28. Bends.

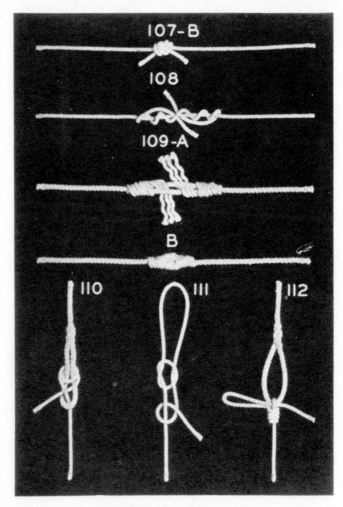

PLATE 29. Bends and other knots.

Plate 29.   BENDS AND OTHER KNOTS

Fig. 107B—The RING GUT or WATER KNOT BEND that was explained on the previous plate is shown here, as it appears when completed and pulled taut.

Fig. 108—A TWISTED BARREL KNOT makes a good dropper attachment for eyed flies. It will hold fast without slipping and at the same time keep the fly extended away from the leader.

Fig. 109A—The ROLLING BARREL KNOT makes an unusually satisfactory tie for joining ends of maitre cord when hanging gill nets. If properly made, it is so smooth that even the finest gill netting will not catch and roll on it. Begin it by unlaying the two ends of the line several turns, then lay them parallel to each other with the ends facing in opposite directions. Now proceed by firmly wrapping the unlayed ends around the body of the line, as illustrated, until two complete turns have been taken on each side. Each end is then brought out between the two parallel lines in the center of the knot. Next, grasp the loose ends of the cord on each side of the knot and pull the knot up by working the slack out of the loose parts, until it comes together in a firm snug fit.

Fig. 109B—After it has been completed, the knot will appear as shown here. It may be rolled under the foot to make it smoother and neater. Trim the ends of the strands as close as possible. If properly made, this knot will never pull out.

Fig. 110—The DOUBLE BECKET HITCH serves a variety of purposes. It has been in use for centuries aboard whaling ships where it is used as a means of attachment for the whale line while making fast to the harpoon becket.

Fig. 111—A WEAVER'S KNOT from Brittany. It was used in this fashion to serve as an adjustment for a loom at an early period. In more recent times, anglers have found practical use for it. It is easily adjusted and conveniently suited for their requirements.

Fig. 112—A SLIPPED HITCH such as this is frequently employed on the belly lines of lifeboat lashings. In this manner, surplus line is neatly done up and disposed of.

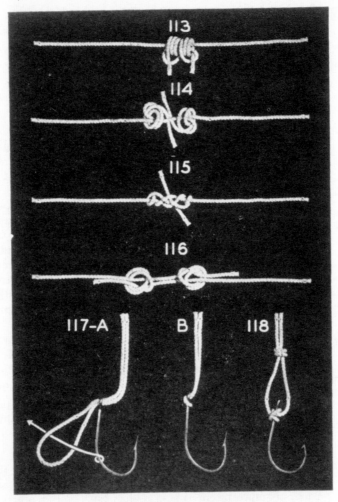

PLATE 30. Line connections and fishhook ties.

Plate 30. LINE CONNECTIONS AND FISHHOOK TIES

Fig. 113—The ROLLING BLOOD KNOT BEND makes a line connection that is dependable.

Fig. 114—The BARREL KNOT BEND variation shown here is another of numerous ways to form this type of tie. It is equally as effective as other methods for making up leaders.

Fig. 115—Shows another way to form a blood knot bend that gives satisfactory use when tied with gut.

Fig. 116—Represents a slight variation of the DOUBLE FISHERMAN'S KNOT, Plate 36, Fig. 155. It is easy to tie and draws up snug and compact.

Fig. 117A—The RING HITCH or TAG KNOT is in reality a lark's head. It is the method by which gangings on codfish trawls are bent to the eyes of hooks. After running the bight on the end of the ganging through the eye of the hook, the hook is then passed through the eye of the bight on the ganging, as indicated.

Fig. 117B—The completed tie with the knot pulled taut.

Fig. 118—The CLOVE HITCH FISHHOOK TIE represents a simple and common method that is universally used by commercial market fishermen when fastening a fishline to a tad hook or, in other words, a hook without an eye.

Plate 31. MISCELLANEOUS FISHHOOK TIES

Fig. 119—The FLY HITCH may be capsized, which automatically transforms it into a figure-of-eight knot.

Fig. 120—The MULTIPLE TWIST FISHHOOK TIE is sometimes erroneously called a reef knot. It may be used to attach leaders to hooks or swivels.

Fig. 121—The FISHHOOK TIE shown here represents another of the many different methods that are used for attaching fishhooks to a line. Its form of construction is clearly illustrated and needs no explanation.

Fig. 122—This represents an old-fashioned but reliable method of attaching a line to a hook. It may be used either on hooks with eyes or flattened hooks without eyes, which are called "tad hooks" by commercial fishermen.

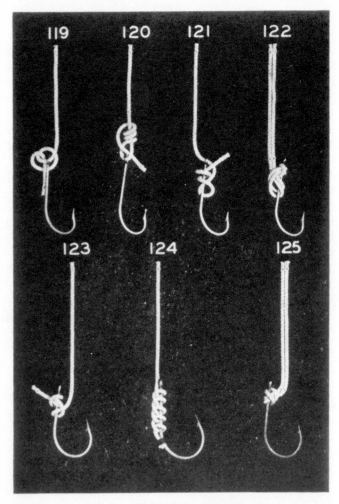

PLATE 31. Miscellaneous fishhook ties.

Fig. 123—Another common form of tie is shown here. It consists of a clove hitch just below the eye of the hook, or below the tad if the hook has no eye. A half hitch is then tied below the clove hitch in the manner illustrated.

Fig. 124—Represents a clumsy-looking but dependable method of hitching the shank of a hook with a line that is first seized to the hook before tying the hitches around the shank in the manner shown. Many hand-line or still fishermen and wharf fishermen also prefer to use this kind of tie for convenience in preference to mastering some of the neater and more conventional forms of ties.

Fig. 125—A simple and practical way of securing a line to a hook is illustrated here.

Plate 32. FISHHOOK TIES

Fig. 126—The COMBINATION OVERHAND KNOT, HALF HITCH FISHHOOK TIE. Like similar knots of simple construction used for the same purpose, it is easily tied without an explanation.

Fig. 127—A FISHERMAN'S KNOT TIE is another simple method of securing a line to a hook.

Fig. 128—A JAMMING REEF KNOT with a blood knot added just above the eye of the fishhook is another typical form of securing a line to a hook.

Fig. 129—A FISHERMAN'S FLY KNOT represents an effective method of attaching a line to a fly. Take a length of colored silk and a hackle from a cock's neck and secure the latter to the hook with a whipping immediately below the eye of the hook, after which run the line through the eye of the hook as shown. This colored line can be joined to another line by the use of a reef knot, as illustrated, above the hook. To form the whipping, take a bight of line and run the ends through the eye of the hook, then lay both ends along the shank of the hook and fold them back toward the eye in the form of a bight. Use only one end of the line—with the other end left inert for the whipping turns—which is stuck through the eye of the bight on the opposite end, after the required amount of turns have been taken. The whipping is then drawn taut from the top end with the inert part of the line.

69

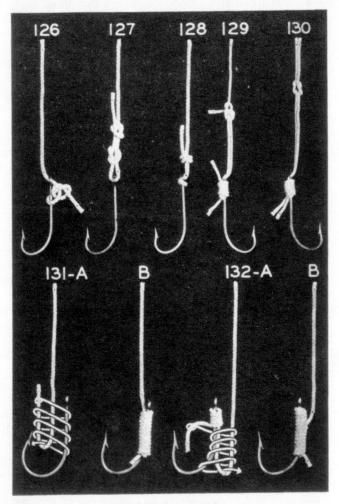

PLATE 32. Fishhook ties.

Fig. 130—The FISHERMAN'S FLY KNOT shown in this illustration is somewhat different from that shown in the previous example, in that the line above the hook is attached to another line by a double sheet bend. The whipping turns are taken with both parts of the line, as indicated, instead of using only one part as in the previous method. Otherwise its formation embraces the same principle.

Fig. 131A—WHIPPING A FISHLINE TO A HOOK, as it is illustrated here, embraces a modern and simple method that is in wide use among numerous fishermen. It is begun by forming a bight in the end of the line, with the standing part next to the hook. Now proceed with the operation by winding the short end of the line around both hook and standing part and over its own part, making as many turns as necessary to bring the whipping down opposite to or just above the barb of the hook. Finish off by sticking the short or working end of the line through the end of the bight and hauling the turns taut.

Fig. 131B—As the completed whipping appears when finished.

Fig. 132A—An earlier method than the previous example, which comes from the renowned angler, Izaak Walton, who lived in the seventeenth century in England. It is made in a manner similar to the modern way except that, in this case, after the bight of line is formed with the standing part on the outside, the short or working end of the line is first wound down the shank of the hook, starting just below the tad end, making three or four turns over its own part to form a collar. The rest of the operation is now continued in the same way, as previously described, with the working end encompassing the hook, its own part and the standing part, as illustrated.

Fig. 132B—This shows the operation completed.

Plate 33. FISHHOOK AND OTHER TIES

Fig. 133A—A FRENCH FISHHOOK TIE of an early period. It comes from Captain Louis Pardiac of Bordeaux, France, who obtained it from Diderot's *Encyclopedia,* Paris, 1747. It was usually applied to hooks with tad ends that were cut square, instead of to the ordinary round ones. The line is clapped on the hook with a hitch about one third of the way below the

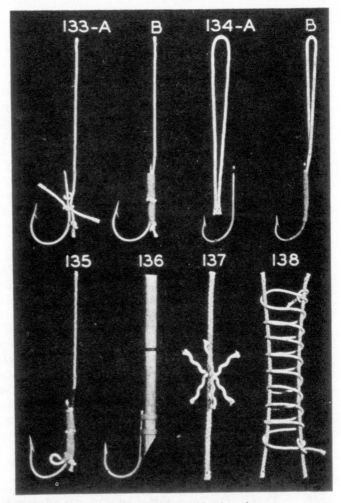

PLATE 33. Fishhook and other ties.

end of the tad. An overhand knot is then tied in the end of the line and it is laid down along the shank, being adjusted so that the end reaches opposite to or just below the barb of the hook. Another short piece of line is now knotted about midway around the standing part and shank of the hook, with the ends tapered and laid along the shank in both directions. The body of the hook is then served with marline, or any suitable line, on each side of the overhand knot.

Fig. 133B—The finished operation.

Fig. 134A—An eye or bight of line may be fastened to a flattened hook, as illustrated here. The size of the eye may be any desired length, with the ends of the line scraped down to a taper to insure a neat, compact, tapered appearance.

Fig. 134B—After the bight of line has been whipped along the shank of the hook, it will appear as shown here. Whippings such as this should have a coat of varnish applied after they are finished.

Fig. 135—COD HOOKS were secured to fishlines in this fashion on the Grand Banks over a century ago. This one is constructed in practically the same manner as the early French method, except the standing part of the line is served from a short way above the collar down to where it is seized to the hook. At the finish the line is tapered and stuck back under four or five turns of serving at the bottom end.

Fig. 136—A HANDMADE GAFF is easily constructed from a large tuna or halibut hook. Hammer the barb against the hook and file it down. Then heat the hook in a flame until it loses its temper and becomes pliable. It may then be bent and shaped into its proper form, with the end of the hook slanting outward slightly more than the illustrated example. The hook is then attached to the handle by sticking the end through a bored hole that is required at the proper place. After this is done the shank of the hook is bent down along the handle. Whippings are applied, as illustrated, to finish off. The end of the hook may also be riveted to the back of the handle for additional security if desired.

Fig. 137—Splicing any line that is accidentally cut or damaged may be accomplished quite easily, so that it will be restored to normal condition and continue to give proficient service. A fishline splice, with the method about to be explained, is

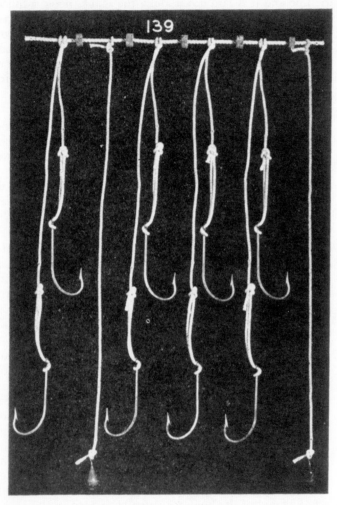

PLATE 34. A surface trawl.

begun by unraveling the threads of the weave a little more than a quarter of an inch on each end. The threads of the exposed ends are then teased out and separated, with about half of them being removed from each end to prevent a bulky joint when they are brought together. Each frayed-out end should now be soaked in warm flytier's wax until the loose material is thoroughly saturated. Each end is next divided into three equal sections and married or interlocked together the same as for an ordinary short splice, which is illustrated here with white line in order to clarify the process. After the ends are joined together, the splice is rolled lightly under the foot in order to insure that the ends lay down on the line in a neat, compact manner without bulging. To finish the operation, bind or wrap the splice with a tight layer of silk thread which is carried just beyond the length of the splice on each side of the line. The binding is secured with a flytier's whip finish or the rodmaker's invisible knot—methods ordinarily used for most any kind of whipped finish on fishlines or rods. After the job has been completed, the splice should be given about two coats of spar varnish to insure a smooth and neat-looking splice which will not weaken the line to any appreciable extent, and will make it only a trifle larger where it is joined together. It will not interfere with the usual functioning of the line in riding through the guides.

Fig. 138—A FISHERMAN'S LITTER such as this may be formed in an emergency with most any suitable objects at hand that will serve the purpose, such as poles, spars, oars or strong pieces of lumber. A piece of rope is wound around whatever is used, in the manner shown, and made fast at each end.

Plate 34. A SURFACE TRAWL

Fig. 139—This represents the principle of construction of a surface trawl which is illustrated here, with only a section of the trawl showing in order to fit the work into the photograph. Gangings such as those shown here are ordinarily spaced from 3½ to 4 feet apart, with cork floats that are disk shaped being used on the headline between each gang-

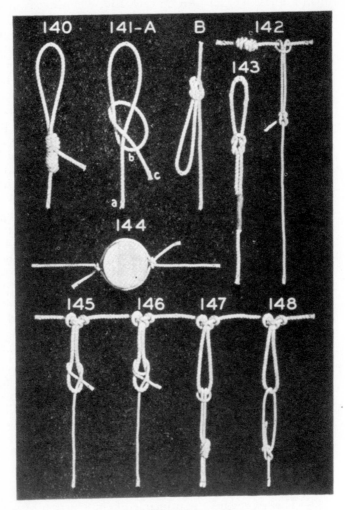

PLATE 35. Miscellaneous ties.

ing. In constructing nets of this type it is customary to make every fourth line an anchor line, from 15 to 25 feet long, which is represented in this case with lead plummets attached to the headline, as shown, with the two longest lines. Surface trawls may vary in length anywhere from 100 feet for the novice to several hundred feet long for the commercial fisherman. Most fishermen prefer to set their trawls in or near tideways, and to return to them at each tide for their catch. When set from shore they are known as "trots" instead of trawls. In this case it is necessary to use only one marker buoy, whereas when the same apparatus is set in open waters it requires two marker buoys, or one for each end, and is then known as a "trawl." See Plate 30, Fig. 117, for the proper way to bend gangings to hooks.

Plate 35. MISCELLANEOUS TIES

Fig. 140—A LINE TO SWIVEL ATTACHMENT may be formed as shown here. A loop is made with the working end of the line laid down along the standing part. It is then wound back over its own part and the standing part with about nine or ten turns, or until it reaches the neck of the loop, then it is stuck down the middle between four or five turns and run out, as illustrated. It is then worked taut and the working end of the line clipped off.

Fig. 141A—A GANGING KNOT such as that shown here is used on trawl lines. This knot is formed by first cutting the required number of short lines an equal length of about $3\frac{1}{2}$ to 4 feet long. They are then hung over anything that is convenient and the knot is begun by forming a loop of approximately the same length in each ganging before the knot is tied. After reaching the stage of the operation shown here, grasp line a and part b with the left hand and turn them back over the loop, at the same time holding line c with the right hand. After this operation has been completed, line c is pulled taut with the right hand while still holding the other parts with the left hand. This automatically secures the tie after the transformation to a ganging has been completed.

77

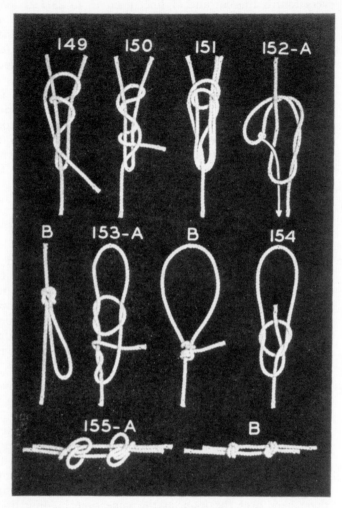

PLATE 36. Gut leader and other ties.

Fig. 141B—The tie is shown here after the previous stages of the operation have been finished. See Plate 30, Fig. 117, for the proper way to bend ganging loops to fishhooks.

Fig. 142—Shows a method by which dropper points may be attached.

Fig. 143—A method by which a permanent loop in the end of a reel line may be bent to a leader by using two loops or the common strap bend is shown here. The end of the fishline on the reel is opened up and frayed out, and a coat of flytier's wax is applied to the loose cord. After this has been accomplished, the end is formed into a loop and whipped against the standing part of the fishline, in the same manner as illustrated here, with large white line.

Fig. 144—A form of tie may be used in this fashion as a slingstone anchor between every three or four hooks on a ground trawl. When stones are used alone for this purpose they are called slingstones. Kellig or killick hitches (Plate 19, Fig. 41) are often used to weight stones to wooden anchors for this same purpose, when bottoms are not too rough and anchors are in no danger of fouling, whereas stones are always used by themselves as anchors on rough or rock bottoms. Ground trawls are ordinarily set at low water and pulled with each tide.

Fig. 145—A SINGLE BECKET HITCH may be used to attach a dropper fly snell to a leader loop in the manner shown.

Fig. 146—A DOUBLE BECKET HITCH serves the same purpose and is more secure.

Fig. 147—A RING HITCH may also be used in this fashion by running the snelled hook through its own loop.

Fig. 148—BOWLINES are sometimes used in attaching dropper fly snells. This is an uncommon yet serviceable form of tie.

Plate 36. GUT LEADER AND OTHER TIES

Fig. 149—The GILL NET KNOT is used for repairing gill nets. Gill nets are subject to hard usage, and often require many repairs after being damaged by severe storms while anchored for fishing.

Fig. 150—Another of the many variations for tying gut leader.

Fig. 151—The GUT LEADER TIE shown here embraces a method

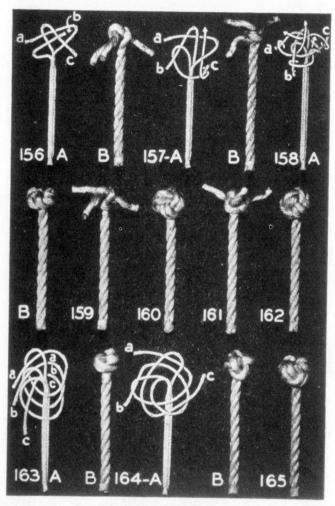

PLATE 37. End rope knots.

for utilizing the bights of two lines together by tying them.

Fig. 152A—A GANGING KNOT (second method). It is often used by fishermen on the Grand Banks to snell their hooks. It is formed by grasping a bight in the line, which is twisted two or three times, as illustrated, then passed under the top part of the line, and down through the opening, parallel with the standing part, as the drawn line indicates. This knot may be employed in the middle of a line, when access to the ends is unavailable.

Fig. 152B—With the bight secured, the knot will then appear as shown here. For the proper method of bending the bight of this tie to the eye of a hook, see Plate 30, Fig. 117.

Fig. 153A—The LEADER LOOP, as shown here, may be employed for casting. However, it is an unusual method and is used much less than the angler's loop. Its method of tying is self-explanatory.

Fig. 153B—A neat, snug knot results when this tie is pulled taut.

Fig. 154—This represents another type of loop for a leader end that is used by some fishermen for casting purposes.

Fig. 155A—The DOUBLE FISHERMAN'S KNOT makes an excellent knot for uniting two lengths of gut when making leader ties.

Fig. 155B—This illustrates the neat, compact finished tie when pulled up snug. If this knot is executed properly it will run through the eyes of a guide without difficulty.

Plate 37. END ROPE KNOTS

Fig. 156A—The THREE-STRAND CROWN KNOT is used to start the preparation of a back splice or as a basis for various other knots. Strand c is brought down over a, then b is brought over c and passed through the bight of a, as indicated by the drawn line. This completes the operation.

Fig. 156B—This shows how the knot appears after each strand has been crowned, as explained in Fig. 156A.

Fig. 157A—The THREE-STRAND WALL KNOT is the opposite of a crown knot. In other words, you wall up and crown down. Each strand of a wall knot comes up through the bight of the strand next to it, whereas each strand of a crown knot goes down through the bight of the next strand. Strand b goes over a and then through the bight of c. Strand c is likewise passed over *b*, and through the bight of *a*, as indicated by the drawn line.

Fig. 157B—This illustration shows the knot as it appears after the operation is complete and the strands have been drawn taut. This knot is used back to back for a shroud knot, in joining two ropes. There are various other uses for it, such as finishing off seizings or forming a basis for other knots. This knot—and all other end rope knots—can be tied with any number of strands by using a repetition of the same key.

Fig. 158A—The THREE-STRAND LANYARD KNOT is tied by making a wall knot first, then passing each strand up through the bight of the following strand and pulling taut after the last pass has been completed. Strand *a* is passed through the bight of *c*, then *b* goes through the bight of *a*, and *c* is likewise tucked through the bight of *b*, as illustrated by the drawn lines.

Fig. 158B—This shows the same knot pulled taut. This is an ideal knot to use as a base for building up other knots, as it pulls up in a neat, uniform manner and holds fast.

Fig. 159—The THREE-STRAND SINGLE MANROPE KNOT has a wall knot as a base, and a crown knot is then tied on top of the wall knot. This provides the framework for a double version of the same knot. In years gone by, it was used to form the cat-o'-nine-tails.

Fig. 160—The THREE-STRAND DOUBLE MANROPE KNOT follows the same method of construction as the single version of this knot, except that the strands are doubled. After the single pass is completed, the knot is doubled by following each pass around on the wall part, then repeating the same procedure on the crown part until the knot is completely doubled. To finish off, work the slack out by pulling the strands up taut. This knot is used on the end of gangway lines and for various other purposes.

Fig. 161—The THREE-STRAND SINGLE STOPPER KNOT includes a crown knot which is formed to start the operation. This is followed by a wall knot around the base. The knot is then pulled taut. However, if it is going to be doubled, enough slack should be left to allow for the additional tucks.

Fig. 162—The THREE-STRAND DOUBLE STOPPER KNOT can likewise be doubled from the single version of this knot by following the same procedure used for the manrope knot. However, the crown part is doubled first instead of the wall part, as in the previous method. Continue by doubling the wall part, as already explained, and then pull the strands up snugly into place. This knot can be used as a stopper on the end of a line, or as a shroud knot, when two of the knots are formed back to back. Almost all other types of end rope knots can be used similarly.

Fig. 163A—The MATTHEW WALKER KNOT at first looks rather difficult to tie, but is really simple when the illustrations are closely followed. Begin by taking the first strand lying nearest the right, which is here designated as strand a. Pass it around the body or standing part of the rope and up under its own part, forming an overhand knot. Then take the next strand, which is designated as strand b, and repeat the same move. The last strand, which is strand c, is then tucked in the same manner. Care should be used in pulling the strands of this knot taut, as each strand should lay around the knot in a uniform manner and in its proper place.

Fig. 163B—When completed, the knot will appear as it does here, after being worked up and pulled taut. This knot is used on the end of rigging lanyards. It will not slip.

Fig. 164A—The THREE-STRAND SINGLE DIAMOND KNOT can be tied by using a number of different keys. The key used in this illustration shows the strands laid out in the form of a flat weave similar to the turk's-head construction. It will be noted that strand a is passed around over c and b, then under b and over c again, and under the bight of b, then under c. Strand b is passed over a and c, then under c and over a, then under the bight of c and passed out underneath a. Strand c is passed over b and a, then under a and over b again, and under the bight of a, then out through b.

Fig. 164B—This shows the knot after it is pulled up taut and the weave is finished. The two-strand version of the knot is used to unite the chin straps of cavalry hats and is sometimes used by boy scouts for the same purpose.

Fig. 165—The THREE-STRAND DOUBLE DIAMOND KNOT follows the same key as illustrated in Plate 38, Fig. 166B, for doubling the strands with additional passes. It will be noted that by continuing each parallel strand around, as they are

83

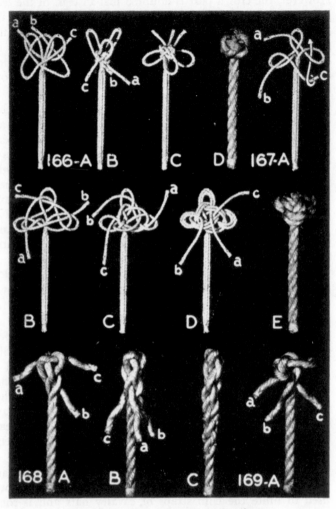

PLATE 38. End rope knots and splices.

illustrated with the first tuck in this key, the weave will produce a double diamond knot, whereas if the weave is split as in Fig. 166C, a sennit knot will be formed.

Plate 38. END ROPE KNOTS AND SPLICES

Fig. 166A—The THREE-STRAND SENNIT KNOT is begun by first tying a diamond knot which has a key, illustrated here, that is different from the preceding method shown in Plate 37, Fig. 164. Strand *a* is passed around and tucked through the bight of *b*. Strand *b* is likewise passed around and tucked through the bight of *c*. Strand *c* is now brought around, as illustrated, and passed through the bight of *a*.

Fig. 166B—This shows the next step of the operation, with strands *a*, *b* and *c* passed down and parallel to the next or following part of the knot that leads down through the weave. This move is necessary in order to convert the diamond knot into a sennit knot. The bights have been purposely pulled out to further clarify the operation.

Fig. 166C—The weave of the knot is continued here, with the illustration of the next or last tuck to finish the operation. After the working ends of the strands have received their last tuck, they will now lead out from underneath the knot and point down. The four-strand weave is next split in the middle and each working strand is now passed over the two following bottom cross strands, then through the center of the weave and out under the two top cross strands. This operation will complete the sennit weave. The bights have also been left pulled out here to help clarify the explanation.

Fig. 166D—This shows the knot as it appears after the slack has been taken out of the bights and the weave has been drawn up neat and snug. White line has been used for the preliminary steps, as in most of the other end rope designs, in order to make the operation as clear as possible. This knot is used in a variety of combinations to form many beautiful rose knot designs.

Fig. 167A—The THREE-STRAND STAR KNOT is a rather difficult knot to explain, but each move in the key, illustrated here, is simplicity itself. Numerous complicated ways of tying the star knot have been called to the authors' attention in by-

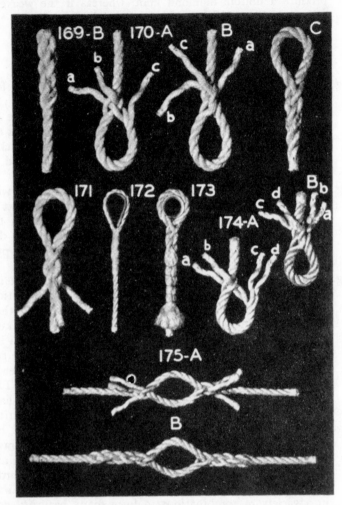

PLATE 39. Eye and cut splices.

gone years. However, this method, which originated in the China Sea, far surpasses any of the other methods of tying this knot. It is a simple, uniform manner of operation that the novice will have no trouble in duplicating if he studies closely the structural design of the knot. It will be noted that the knot is begun by laying out an underhand eye with each strand, then the end of the line of the next or adjoining strand is passed through the eyes in the manner illustrated.

Fig. 167B—The next step in the formation of the knot is shown here, the working ends being designated as *a, b* and *c*. They have each been passed over the top of the knot and out through each following eye.

Fig. 167C—The parts underneath are now doubled by passing the working ends around and up through the eyes. The working ends of the strands are rotated around the body of the knot as they are passed from right to left, and care should be taken to observe the structural formaton of the pattern that is assuming shape at this point. The top parts of the knot are now doubled like the bottom parts, completing the next step in the operation. There is only one more series of passes to make from this point in order to finish the knot.

Fig. 167D—The last move is shown here, the working ends being brought back parallel around each eye in the opposite direction from the general trend of the weave. This pass will double the eyes. The ends now come out through the center of the knot as shown. This series of illustrations has purposely been laid out flat to help clarify the construction, but of course in actual practice the knot is formed on top of the rope and not on the side, as shown here.

Fig. 167E—The completed STAR KNOT as it appears after being worked up and pulled taut, with the ends cut off short on top of the knot. As a rule, a lanyard knot is used as a base on which to form this type of knot, although these illustrations omit the lanyard knot in order to make the construction appear less complicated. This is one of the most popular of decorative knots that were tied by the old-time shellbacks. It makes a beautiful design when tied with six parts instead of three, as shown here. The same key is used in the making of this knot, regardless of the number of strands.

Fig. 168A—The THREE-STRAND BACK SPLICE is begun with a crown knot. Then each strand is tucked over the next strand and under the second strand. In this illustration, strands *a* and *c* have not yet been tucked, while strand *b* has received one tuck. The splicing is continued by tucking strands *a* and *c* in the prescribed manner.

Fig. 168B—This shows the splice after strands *a*, *b* and *c* have each been tucked once or, in other words, one round of tucks has been completed. Make several tucks, and taper the splice down by splitting each strand in half for each remaining tuck. Then pull taut and trim all strands.

Fig. 168C—This shows the splice as it will appear when finished. This splice may be tapered or left untapered. However, three or four rounds of tucks should be made if the strands are going to be cut off without being tapered.

Fig. 169A—The THREE-STRAND SAILMAKER'S BACK SPLICE begins with a crown knot as in the regular splice. But instead of going over one and under one, each tuck is made over, around, and then under the next, or following strand, which brings them out with the lay of the rope. Strands *a*, *b* and *c* have each received one tuck in this illustration. The bight of strand *b* has been left pulled out in order to give a clearer picture of the way the strands are tucked. This splice is worked down and finished off in the same manner as in the preceding method. Sailmakers use this neat form of splicing for awnings. Illustration 169B, showing the completed splice, will be found on Plate 39.

Plate 39.   EYE AND CUT SPLICES

Fig. 169B—This shows the finished splice that was explained in Plate 38, Fig. 169A.

Figs. 170A, B and C—The THREE-STRAND EYE SPLICE is made as follows: Unlay the rope a sufficient distance, and make an eye of the required size; tuck the bottom strand under one strand against the lay, and place the middle strand under the next strand in the same manner. Turn the splice over and tuck the remaining strand as previously described in Fig. 168. Strands *a* and *b* are shown tucked in Fig. 170A. Fig. 170B shows the splice turned over, with strand *c* tucked.

Tuck each strand against the lay a second time, over one and under one, and repeat as many times as desired. After tapering down to finish off, the splice will appear as in Fig. 170C. This splice and all other splices can be rolled under the foot or hammered down to insure a neat, close-fitting job.

Fig. 171—The THREE-STRAND SAILMAKER'S EYE SPLICE is begun by unlaying the rope and making the first tucks as though for the regular eye splice. Then continue by making the sailmaker's tucks (see Fig. 169A) until the required number has been made. The splice is tapered down and the strands are cut off short to finish. This shows the splice after the first set of sailmaker's tucks has been completed.

Fig. 172—In the EYE SPLICE SERVED, the eye is bent around a thimble, then spliced in, tapered down and served in the usual manner. A thimble is used to prevent a hook from chafing the rope.

Fig. 173—The ROUND THIMBLE EYE SPLICE with ends frayed is a round thimble spliced into an eye with the ends frayed out and hitched along the body of the rope with marline.

Figs. 174A and B—The FOUR-STRAND EYE SPLICE is a repetition of the three-strand method, except at the beginning. The bottom strand is tucked under two strands, and the other strands are tucked under one each. Strand *a* in Fig. 174A is shown tucked under two strands as described, and strand *b* under one strand. Turn the splice over and tuck strands *c* and *d* accordingly. The splice will then appear as in Fig. 174B. Continue by tucking over one and under one against the lay, until the required number of tucks has been made.

Fig. 175A—The CUT SPLICE is made by measuring off the required distance, depending on the size of the eye desired. Then splice each end into the standing part of the other rope. This illustration shows the first set of tucks with the end of each adjoining rope.

Fig. 175B—Shows the completed splice. The splice is used to form an eye or collar in the bight of a rope.

Plate 40. SHORT AND LONG SPLICES

Fig. 176A—The THREE-STRAND SHORT SPLICE is the strongest and most secure method of uniting two ropes. It is stronger than

89

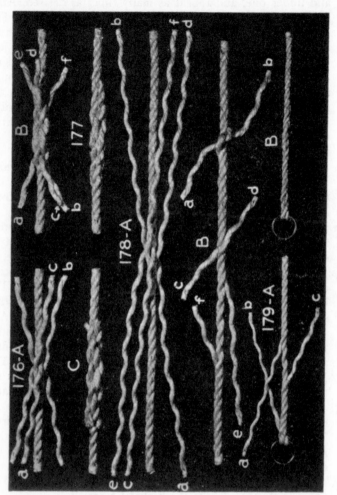

PLATE 40. Short and long splices.

the long splice, but increases the diameter of the rope, so that the spliced portion of the rope may be unable to pass over the sheave of a block. To begin this splice, unlay the ends of each rope, and marry the strands, as shown in the illustration. In marrying a rope, one strand of one rope comes between two strands of the other, as shown by strand *a*, which comes between the two strands *b* and *c*. The work will be found much simpler to execute if a temporary seizing is placed at the point where both ropes have been married. This will serve to hold the ropes in position until the first tucks are made. The strands on the right-hand side are, for the moment, left alone. Begin with any strand on the left. Tuck it over one and under one against the lay.

Fig. 176B—After strands *a*, *b* and *c* have been tucked, strands *d*, *e* and *f* are tucked once each. The splice is begun on both sides, there now being one round of tucks. Two more tucks are put in with each strand, making three rounds of tucks in all, which is the proper amount for a secure splice.

Fig. 176C—This shows the Short Splice after two rounds of tucks have been made. After another round of tucks has been finished, the splice is then rolled under the foot and pounded down with a fid or mallet to make it round and work the strands into place. The strands are then cut off, but not too close, or they may work out when tension is applied. The splice may be tapered by following directions in Plate 38, Fig. 168A.

Fig. 177—The Three-Strand Sailmaker's Short Splice is begun by marrying the strands of each rope. Choose any two strands lying next to each other, in order to have one adjacent strand from each rope. Then, instead of going over one and under one, as in the common splice, tuck them around one another. As there is a right and wrong way of tucking these strands in the sailmaker's splices, the following method should be followed to eliminate the possibility of making any errors: When the strands have been married, each set of adjoining strands is tied together by forming an overhand knot with the lay of the rope, or in the same manner as in finishing off a long splice. The splice is now continued by tucking each strand over, around, and then under the next or following strand in the standing part of the rope, which

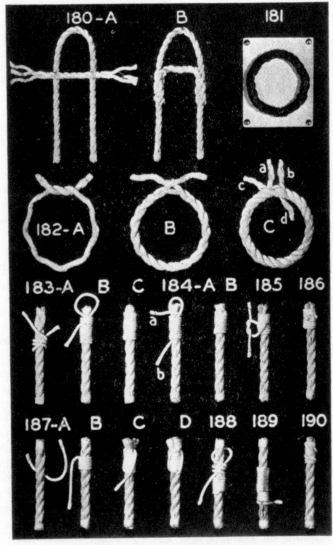

PLATE 41. Splices, grommets and whippings.

brings them out with the lay of the rope after each tuck. This method is repeated until three rounds of tucks have been made. (The illustrated example has been tapered down after one round of tucks to fit into the limited space.)

Fig. 178A—The THREE-STRAND LONG SPLICE (over and under style), though weaker than the short splice and requiring more rope, does not increase the diameter of the rope appreciably and therefore can be run over a sheave or pulley without jamming in the block. To begin, unlay the strands of both ropes four or five times farther than in a short splice. (In reality, the strands are unlaid much farther than shown in the illustration, since it was necessary to make the splice shorter in order to get the work into the photograph.) Then marry the strands as shown here, and group them off into pairs. The next step is to take strand *a* and unlay it a short distance. Then take its mate, strand *b*, and lay it into the groove that was made when strand *a* was removed. When strand *b* has been laid up to strand *a*, and they meet, tie an overhand knot with both strands to hold them temporarily. Next, go back to the center and knot strands *c* and *d* together, so they will remain where they are. Take strand *f* and unlay it to the left the same distance that strand *a* was unlaid to the right. Then lay strand *e* into the groove left when strand *f* was taken out.

Fig. 178B—This shows how the splice looks after the preceding steps have been taken. (The overhand knots have been tied with only one set of strands in this illustration.) Join strands *a* and *b* together on the right, with an overhand knot; strands *c* and *d* are joined together in the center. Strand *f* has been unlaid, and strand *e* is being laid into the groove until it reaches strand *f*. The next and final step is the disposal of the ends of each set of strands after they have been joined together with an overhand knot, tied with the lay of the rope, as illustrated by strands *a* and *b*. This is done by splicing each one of the separate ends over and under against the lay of the rope with a sufficient number of tucks which can be tapered at the end. The procedure of finishing off a splice of this type can be accomplished in several ways, but the method explained here is probably the most commonly used. The four-strand long splice is prepared in the same manner

as the three-strand method, except that the operation requires an additional allowance for the extra strands after
the two ropes have been married. In other words, each set of
strands must be laid up and joined together an equal distance apart. They are then finished in the regular manner.

Figs. 179A and B—The CHAIN SPLICE is tied as follows: Unlay
the rope a considerable distance and reeve strands b and c
through the end link of the chain; then unlay strand a quite
some distance down the rope; tuck strand b under strand c,
and lay up strand c in the groove vacated by strand a. Join
them together with an overhand knot, disposing of the
strands by tucking against the lay, as in a regular long splice,
with strand b also tucked over and under against the lay to
finish. Fig. 179A illustrates the open splice at the beginning
and Fig. 179B shows how it looks when complete.

Plate 41.   SPLICES, GROMMETS AND WHIPPINGS

Figs. 180A and B—The HORSESHOE SPLICE is begun by unlaying
a short piece of rope, as shown in Fig. 180A, and splicing it
into the standing parts of another piece of rope which has
been bent in horseshoe fashion. The completed splice will
then appear as in Fig. 180B. This splice was formerly used
to separate the legs of a pair of shrouds.

Fig. 181—This illustration shows a HEMP-LAID LONG-SPLICED
GROMMET. A single strand of tarred hemp is laid up into 3
strands. When the strand is laid up 2 turns, cross the strand
from the left or inside the strand from the right, then continue around until the strands meet again and tie an overhand knot. Next, unlay the strands at the overhand knot by
a half turn, to make them flat, then continue by tucking
the ends with a tapered sailmaker's splice.

Fig. 182A—The THREE-STRAND GROMMET represents a type of
ropework that can be utilized for making many different articles, such as strops, chest handles, and quoits. It is made
from a single strand of rope, as follows: First, take a piece of
rope of the desired thickness; determine the circumference of
the grommet you wish to make, then measure off $3\frac{1}{2}$ times
this circumference. (In other words, if the circumference is 1
foot, $3\frac{1}{2}$ feet is the proper measurement.) Next, cut the

rope and unlay one strand. Tie an overhand knot in this strand with the lay of the rope, as shown in the illustration. (The strands have purposely been left short, in order to fit them into the photograph.)

Fig. 182B—Begin by laying up one strand or, if desired, the ends of both sides of the overhand knot can be laid up at the same time, which will produce the same result. When the ends meet, there will be a grommet of two strands, as shown here.

Fig. 182C—Continue the strand around again, making a three-strand grommet, as illustrated here. When the strands meet again at the finish, halve them and tie an overhand knot, then proceed to dispose of the ends, as in the common long splice. In this case, strands *a* and *b* represent the inactive half of the strands which will be tucked into the grommet, while strands *c* and *d* are the parts with which the overhand knot is formed. They are also tucked into the grommet to finish off.

Fig. 183A—A PLAIN WHIPPING. (Whippings are always made with the twine wound against the lay of the rope. It is also customary to work the turns toward the end of the rope.) Fig. 183A shows the beginning of the whipping. One end of the twine is placed near the end of the rope, and then run back a short distance before the turns are made.

Fig. 183B—After the desired number of turns has been wound around the rope, the end of the twine is laid in the direction shown in this illustration. Then three or four more turns are wound around the end of the rope with the bight of the twine.

Fig. 183C—After the finishing turns have been wound around, as just described, the last turn is drawn taut, and both ends are cut off close to finish the whipping.

Fig. 184A—The TEMPORARY WHIPPING is made by first laying a bight on the rope a short distance from the end. A number of turns are taken about the rope and on top of the bight. End *a* of the whipping twine is put through the loop, and end *b*, which forms the bight, is drawn until the loop is under the turns. Both ends of the twine are then cut off close.

Fig. 184B—This figure shows the whipping after the ends have been cut off short to finish the whipping.

Fig. 185—The AMERICAN WHIPPING, called by this name in England, is a variation of the plain whipping. Both ends of the twine are brought up in the middle of the turns and joined with a reef knot. The reef knot should be made in the groove between two strands of the rope, so that it can be pushed down between them, beneath the turns. In this case, the bottom part of the reef knot has been pulled down under the turns, but the top part of the knot has not yet been pulled up taut.

Fig. 186—The ORDINARY WHIPPING is similar to the American Whipping, except that instead of joining the ends of the twine with a reef knot that is pulled up underneath the turns, the reef knot in this method is left tightly knotted on top of the turns. The ends are then cut off close to the knot to finish the operation.

Fig. 187A—The PALM AND NEEDLE WHIPPING at first appears to be rather difficult, but it is actually one of the simplest types of whippings. First, take a suitable length of twine, then thread it in a sail needle and wax it well. Proceed by stitching it through the rope, as shown here.

Fig. 187B—Next, take the proper number of turns around the rope and the short end of the twine, keeping each turn as taut as possible.

Fig. 187C—When enough turns have been taken, the twine is stitched through the rope again. Then bring the twine down on top of the turns, giving it the proper position along the lay of the rope. It is next stitched under another strand and brought back up again over the top of the turns. This operation is repeated three times, until all the grooves between the rope strands have strands of the twine resting in them.

Fig. 187D—Finally, an additional stitch is taken through the rope with the twine, which is then cut off. The whipping, if properly made, will look like this illustration.

Note: Very few people know the proper length to make a whipping. Some keep winding turns around the rope until it "looks right." But this is not a dependable method. A whipping should be as long as the diameter of the rope upon which it is placed. In the illustrations, large white line has been used purposely, and an exceptional number of turns has been taken in order to clarify the pictures. Sail twine is the most commonly used material for work of this sort.

Fig. 188—The PLAIN WHIPPING in the middle of a line serves a special purpose. In most cases, a whipping is used to prevent the end of a rope from fraying out or becoming unlaid. But it sometimes becomes necessary to place a whipping in the center of a rope or other object. In order to do this, leave several turns slack, and pass the end of the whipping twine under them, as shown. Each turn is then hove taut, and the end pulled to take out the slack.

Fig. 189—The SEAMAN'S WHIPPING is made in the following way: First, take a piece of waxed sail twine of the required length, then lay one end of this along the rope's end to be whipped and, while holding it in place under the thumb, wind the twine tightly around it and the rope. These turns are continued until near the end of the rope; then lay another piece of twine in the form of a bight along the rope's end, and take about four more whipping turns over this twine. The end of the line is then passed through the eye of its bight. The bight is pulled from under the turns, at the same time heaving the end of the twine up snug and tight under the whipping turns. This is an excellent method for securing the end of the line under the turns, as it leaves no excess slack to work out at the finish. The illustration shows the end of the whipping line passed through the eye of the bight, prior to its being pulled through under the turns.

Fig. 190—The FRENCH or GRAPEVINE WHIPPING is a very secure and unique method of whipping the end of a rope. A suitable length of whipping twine is taken, and an overhand knot is tied a short distance back from the end of the rope. Next, a continuous row of half hitches is put on against the lay of the rope, until the end is almost reached. Then two loose hitches are taken, and the end of the twine is placed under them; the hitches are drawn taut and the slack end pulled to complete the whipping.

Plate 42. WHIPPINGS AND SEIZINGS

Fig. 191A—The SAILMAKER'S WHIPPING is made as follows: The end of the rope is opened for a short distance; a bight of the twine is put around one strand, leading the ends be-

97

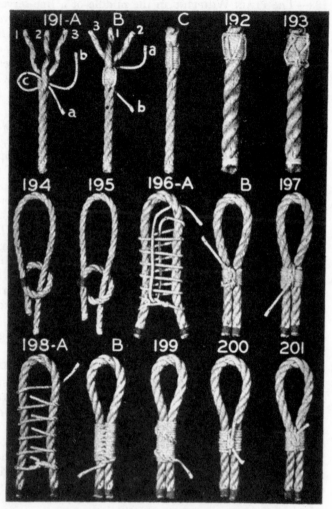

PLATE 42. Whippings and seizings.

tween the other two strands, as shown in the illustration. End *a*, in this case, is the moving end, and end *b* is the standing end. The strands are next laid up again, and the proper number of turns taken around the rope. Then bight *c* is brought up and passed over the end of Strand 1.

Fig. 191B—This illustration shows the whipping after bight *c* has been passed over Strand 1. It is next heaved tight by the standing end of the twine, and the standing end is carried up alongside Strand 3. Then the working and standing ends are knotted tightly together between the strands and cut off.

Fig. 191C—This shows the whipping after it is finished. The end of the rope has been seized on top of the whipping for clearness, but ordinarily the strands are trimmed close to the top part of the work.

Fig. 192—Snaking is an old method of securing a whipping or seizing on a heavy rope or cable. When as many turns have been placed on the rope as desired, put the sail needle through the rope and haul the twine taut. The working end is then taken over and under the upper and lower turns of the whipping, as shown.

Fig. 193—The HERRINGBONE WHIPPING is somewhat similar to the whipping just described, except that when the twine is put through the upper and lower turns of the whipping, they are half-hitched rather than merely stitched through.

Fig. 194—The OUTSIDE CLINCH SEIZING is a running knot formed by reeving the standing part of the rope through the eye of a simple clinch seizing.

Fig. 195—The INSIDE CLINCH is similar in method to the preceding, except that it is somewhat more secure. When hauled taut around a spar or other object, it jams on itself. While it is somewhat more difficult to release than the outside clinch, it is a good knot to use when a turn is to be taken about an object and, after being drawn taut, must be slipped rather quickly. These clinches, Figs. 194 and 195, have a single cross seizing.

Figs. 196A and B—The FLAT SEIZING is used only as a light seizing, when the strain is not too great and there is equal tension on the two parts or ropes to be seized together. First, take a sufficient length of marline or seizing twine and splice an eye in one end. Then place it around both of the ropes or shrouds and pass the unspliced end through its own eye, heaving it taut. Take the required number of turns, passing the end of the seizing line beneath the turns and between the two parts being seized together, then out through the eye of the seizing line, as shown in Fig. 196A. Next, take a round turn with the seizing line, passing it between the lines and over the turns already made, and heaving it taut. Then pass the seizing line around again, making two turns before finishing off with a braided clove hitch, as illustrated in Fig. 196B. These additional turns are called "frapping turns."

Fig. 197—The ROUND SEIZING is stronger than the flat seizing and is to be preferred where the strain is very pronounced. Begin as in the flat version, but make an odd number of passes (say, seven or nine) before reeving the end of the seizing line beneath the turns and back through its own eye; then heave taut. These turns make up the first layer and are called the "lower turns." Next, the top or upper turns are made with an even number of passes (one less than the lower turns), which places the upper turns in the grooves formed between the lower ones. The end of the seizing line is then tucked under the last of the lower turns and hove taut.

Figs. 198A and B—The RACKING or NIPPERED SEIZING is the best method to use when an unequal strain is placed on two shrouds, as when turning in a deadeye. The seizing line should be well stretched before being used in a seizing of this type. Begin, as in the flat or round seizing, by forming a turn around the two parts to be seized, then reeving the end of the seizing line through its own eye. The turns are started in a sort of figure-of-eight fashion, as illustrated. After making about ten passes (if the strain is to be severe), start the second passes back in the direction of the beginning, fitting them in between the grooves left by the first turns. Finish off by reeving the end of the seizing line through its own eye again. Then tie an overhand knot and cut off short. A slightly different method of making this seizing can be used if desired. Before starting the second turns or passes, form a half hitch on the inside of the last figure-of-eight loop, and then follow back toward the beginning, as already described. The cross or frapping turns may also be applied to finish off.

Fig. 199—The FRENCH or GRAPEVINE SEIZING is an ornamental type of seizing, made by half-hitching one strand around the body of the seized parts. It is started by overlapping one strand with the working part, and can be finished either by tying an overhand knot up close or by tucking the end under.

Fig. 200—The NECKLACE SEIZING is begun in the same way as the racking seizing, by taking the required number of figure-of-eight turns, then tucking the end of the seizing line under the last turn and across the front to form a reef knot with the line from the other side.

Fig. 201—The MIDDLE SEIZING closely follows the temporary whipping, Plate 41, Fig. 184, except that the bottom strand forming the loop is cut off short. Then the other end of the seizing line, after being rove through the eye of the loop on the opposite side, is passed around the seizing two times to form the cross or frapping turns. The seizing is finished off with a reef knot, as illustrated.

Plate 43. ROPE COILS AND GASKETS

Fig. 202—The BULKHEAD HITCH shown here is used for suspending rope coils over a peg or any other suitable object. The way the line is done up is quite obvious.

Fig. 203—The SIMPLE ROPE COIL HITCH shown here is an easy and common method of doing up a line.

Fig. 204—The ROPE COIL HITCH, second method, is slightly different from the preceding method, as can be observed from the illustration.

Fig. 205—To FLEMISH DOWN A COIL OF ROPE, the coil must be laid down so that each succeeding fake lies outside of the other. Begin at the center of the coil and work outward, so that each fake lies flat on the deck in a concentric coil. In coiling rope in this manner, it is the practice to lay down right-handed rope in a right-hand coil, that is, the rope is laid down from left to right—clockwise, or with the sun. The opposite is the case with left-handed rope. It is laid down from right to left—counterclockwise, or against the sun. In all coils of this type, it is important that the running

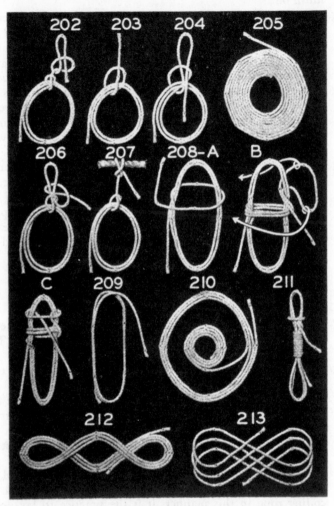

PLATE 43. Rope coils and gaskets.

part of the coil be in the center, while the end of the line is on the outside. This is done to insure free running.

Fig. 206—The COIL HITCH is used for doing up tackles. It is similar to Fig. 204 except that it has an additional hitch around the eye.

Fig. 207—The BULKHEAD HITCH, second method. The line is secured to whatever object it is going to be attached to, in the manner shown in the illustration.

Figs. 208A and B—MAKING UP A GASKET. When sails are taken in on sailing vessels, they are lashed to the yards with ropes which are called "gaskets." When under sail, the gaskets are, of course, not in use, and therefore must be coiled up in a fashion that will permit them to be released instantly when so desired. A gasket is made in the following manner: Take the bight of the gasket about four feet from the end which is made fast. Now begin coiling it up in the hand, as shown in Fig. 208A. When the entire line has been coiled, it is flattened out; but be careful that none of the bights in the coil are dropped out of the hand. Next, take several turns around the coil with the standing end. The bight of the standing end is now passed through the upper portion of the coil and then passed over the top of all the bights, as shown by the drawn line in Fig. 208B. The working end, in this case, is left free in order to make the illustration clear, but in actual use it forms part of the standing end which is made fast.

Fig. 208C—This shows the gasket after the bight has been brought to rest, which automatically converts it to inside hitches as it is securely adjusted to make the coil fast.

Fig. 209—To COIL DOWN ROPE is to lay it down right-handed or left-handed, as the lay of the rope requires, with one fake directly over the fake below it. The coil is then capsized to insure free running.

Fig. 210—To FLEMISH DOWN A COIL OF ROPE, second method, as illustrated here, two flat concentric coils are formed, with the first or inside coil serving as a heart, around which the rope is then coiled as an outside layer, in the manner shown.

Fig. 211—The HEAVING LINE or SASH CORD COIL is practically the same as a gasket shortening, except that it is started from a lower position near the opposite end and the line is put

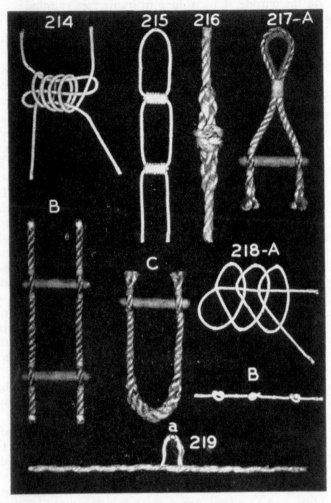

PLATE 44. Rope ladder making.

through the center of the coil at the beginning. The round turns are then taken on top instead of on the bottom of each other, as in the gasket method. Otherwise, it is finished the same way.

Fig. 212—The OVERLAPPING FIGURE-OF-EIGHT COIL is simply a Flemish coil in which two of the opposite sides are overlapped after the coil has been laid down.

Fig. 213—FAKING DOWN HAWSERS is sometimes done in the manner illustrated. The first step is to lead the line out, removing all kinks and twists. Then begin by winding the rope, at its secured end, in a crisscross manner, each fake being placed directly over the fake below it.

Plate 44.   ROPE LADDER MAKING

Fig. 214—The LADDER RUNG KNOT is tied with two parts of rope. One part is laid out with a bight at each end. The other part is passed through the top bight on the right, as shown. Any number of round turns can be taken, suitable to the length of the rung. The rope is then passed through the lower bight on the left, and the knot is pulled taut.

Fig. 215—In the ROPE LADDER shown here, the rope rungs are made as in Fig. 214. For every other rung, the knot is reversed by forming it the opposite way.

Fig. 216—The WALL or AMERICAN SHROUD KNOT is made as follows: Unlay the rope for a suitable length and marry the ends; then form a wall knot on each side with each set of three strands, the strands going with the lay. The ends are then spliced into the standing part. This type of knot can be formed with any kind of suitable tie, such as a diamond, manrope or stopper knot, which also are formed back to back in the same way. It was used in the days before the introduction of wire rigging to repair shrouds that had been shot away in action.

Figs. 217A, B and C—In the STERN ROPE LADDER with wooden rungs, the rungs are always spaced about 12 inches apart. If the ladder is to be from 24 to 25 feet long, it will require about two dozen rungs, each one a foot long, with the ends scored according to the size of the rope being used. After stretching and laying out the proper amount of rope, middle

105

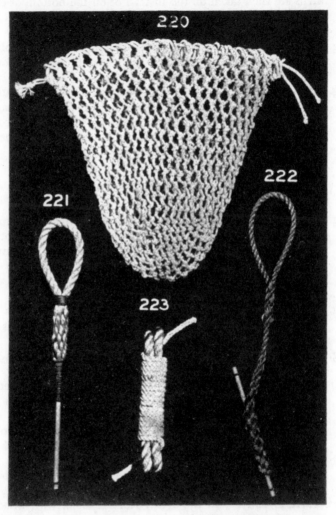

PLATE 45. A shrimp net, harpoon lashings and fender.

it and seize it around a thimble. Then mark off, on both parts of the rope, the place intended for each rung. Beginning at the end nearest the thimble, open the rope up with a fid and push a rung in. Repeat on the opposite side, and continue until all the rungs are placed. Then, using a seven- or eight-turn whipping, seize the rope on both sides just above and below each rung. Splice both the ends together to finish the operation. Fig. 217A represents the top part, whereas Figs. 217B and C show the middle and bottom parts, respectively. It was necessary to illustrate the ladder in three sections because of the limited space.

Figs. 218A and B—In the TRICK CHAIN OF OVERHAND KNOTS, the hitches are laid out in the fashion shown in Fig. 218A. Then the end of the line is passed through the hitches and pulled taut, bringing the knots out as they appear in Fig. 218B.

Fig. 219—TAKING A ROPE YARN OUT OF A STRAND. It is surprising how few people know how to execute such a simple operation as taking a rope yarn out of a strand. The method commonly used is to extract it from the end. The proper method is to grasp the yarn, *a*, from the center of the strand, and then withdraw it.

Plate 45.   A SHRIMP NET, HARPOON LASHINGS AND FENDER

Fig. 220—A SHRIMP NET is made in a manner similar to the landing net, except that, in this case, a draw cord is employed through the first row of double meshes, with which to close the mouth of the net.

Fig. 221—The HARPOON LASHING, first method, is used on the end of a harpoon, when there is no metal ring in which a line may be secured. First, take a suitable length of rope, middle it, and put on a seizing, forming an eye. Unlay the strands and the yarns, and lay up the yarns again to form two yarn nettles. The seizing of the eye is next placed on the end of the harpoon, and the nettles laid down along the shaft. With a good strong piece of marline, cross-point the harpoon shaft for a distance of six inches (or more, depending on the length of the harpoon). The nettles are finally scrape-tapered and marled down on the shaft.

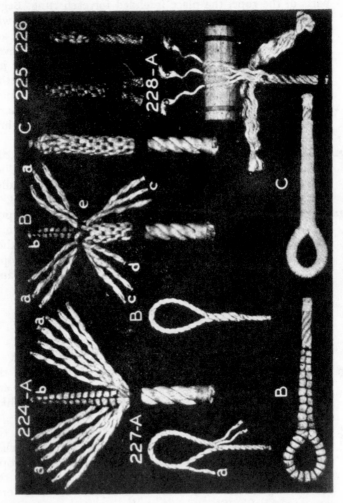

PLATE 46. Rope pointing, Flemish and spindle eyes.

Fig. 222—The HARPOON LASHING, second method, is made in the same manner as the knot shown in Fig. 221, except that when the strands return to the beginning they are spliced into the standing part, instead of being passed back through the body of the knot. An eye is spliced into the other end of the standing part into which the harpoon line is secured. By inserting the shaft of a harpoon into this knot, it automatically jams on itself, and the knot must then be pushed together in order to free the harpoon.

Fig. 223—A FISHERMAN'S FENDER such as this would be frowned upon by the old time shellback, but fishermen often find this makeshift arrangement satisfactory enough to use as a fender. Any kind of an old worn hawser is suitable to use for the turns that comprise the body. It is served over with a small rope, in the manner illustrated. To finish off, reeve each opposite end of the small rope through the ends of the larger rope which forms the body of the fender.

Plate 46. ROPE POINTING, FLEMISH AND SPINDLE EYES

Fig. 224A—The COMMON ROPE POINTING is one of the best methods of finishing off the end of a rope to prevent the strands from fraying. It also stiffens the end of the rope so that it can be passed through a block easily. To start the work, clap a stout seizing on the rope about ten inches back from its end. Unlay the strands and make enough nettles to cover the rope completely. These nettles are shown in the illustration at a. There should always be an even number of nettles; in this case, twelve. The remaining yarns are then tapered by scraping, after which they are marled together securely, as shown at b. Next, pass each alternate nettle down and the remainder up, laying the latter along the conical center. At the point where the two groups of nettles separate, take two turns around the upright nettles and the cone with a piece of marline, securing the second turn with a half hitch. Next, bring the vertical nettles down on the standing part of the rope and the other nettles up along the center. The marline is again brought up and two turns taken about the now vertical nettles and the cone, after which the last turn of the marline is again secured with a half hitch. Repeat this

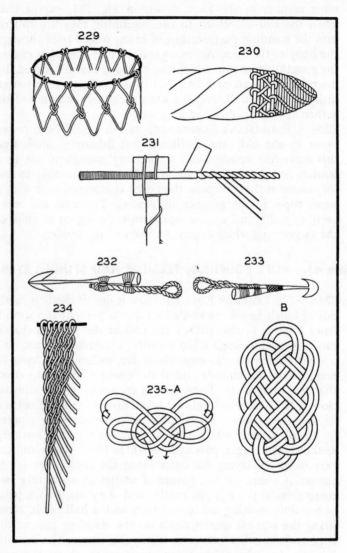

PLATE 47. Miscellaneous knotwork.

sequence of operations until the desired length has been reached. A blood knot can also be used with marline, instead of a half hitch, to stop the nettles around the core as this form of tie holds hard and fast for an operation of this nature, and it is probably more secure than a half hitch.

Fig. 224B—Do not stop all of the nettles involved in the work in order to finish it off, but take three loose turns around the one set of nettles and the core. Next, take each nettle from the second group and bring it up over the turns of marline and then back underneath them, as shown at d. The nettles shown at c have not been tucked. When all of the nettles of the second group have been tucked, as explained, the turns of the marline are brought up taut. All of the ends of the nettles are cut off and the work will look as shown in Fig. 224C. The core has been purposely left intact in this illustration to make the work easier to understand, but in actual practice it is also cut off, after working the point down as far as possible.

Fig. 225—Represents an ORDINARY EYE POINTING. Form the eye and place a seizing around the two parts of rope, then unlay the strands and select the outside yarns, which are laid back and tied to the body of the rope. Taper the strands forming the heart and marl them down in the usual manner. Make two round turns with marline to start the pointing, after laying each alternate pair of yarns back and the others down. Continue with another pair of round turns, bringing each alternate pair of yarns down and the others back with each additional pass. Whip the end securely to finish the job.

Fig. 226—An ORDINARY ROPE POINTING done in the same manner as the work illustrated in Fig. 225.

Fig. 227A—The FLEMISH EYE SPLICE, which is a little different from the common eye splice, can be used when there is a tendency for the eye to spread apart. First, unlay the rope a sufficient length for turning in a common eye splice. Select one of the three strands and unlay it until the remaining two strands are long enough to form an eye of the desired size. Bend these two strands down until they meet the single strand, a, again. Instead of laying strand a upon the standing part, lay it in the other direction, beginning a short distance from the end of the opened strands.

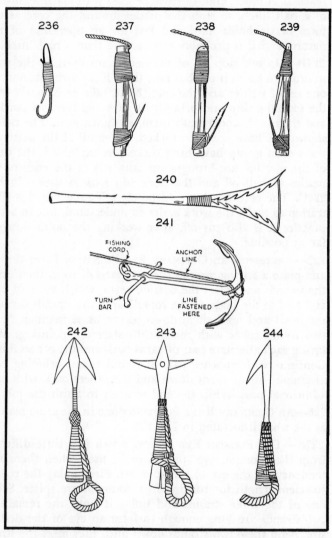

236 237 238 239

240

241

FISHING CORD

ANCHOR LINE

TURN BAR

LINE FASTENED HERE

242 243 244

PLATE 48. Emergency fishhook ties, whaling irons, etc.

Fig. 227B—When strand *a* has been laid up again, proceed to dispose of the ends, as in the common splice. In this illustration, the strands were tucked by using the sailmaker's method, which brings the strands through the rope and along the lay in a uniform manner.

Figs. 228A, B and C—An ARTIFICIAL or SPINDLE EYE in four-strand Manila rope. Place a whipping at a distance from the end of the rope about equal to three times the rope's circumference. Unlay the strands back as far as the whipping and separate them into yarns, which are to be divided into two equal groups. There are two ways in which this eye can be formed. The yarns either can be knotted together or they can be laid up into nettles and then knotted together around a spar having a diameter equal to twice the circumference of the rope. Take care not to make all of the overhand knots, or double overhand knots for added security, at one place around the spar; instead, space them equally distant from each other. After all of the yarns have been knotted together, lay them down around the eye and on the standing part of the rope. Next, take a length of marline and bind the knotted yarns with marline hitches all around the eye. Scrape and taper the ends of the yarns down on the standing part of the rope and marl them in the same manner as the eye. The eye and the standing part are then served, or the eye can be parceled before serving, to make a neat job. Fig. 228A shows the first stage of the work, and Fig. 228B as it looks when marled. Fig. 228C shows the completed eye.

This type of eye is used for the collars of stays and was used also for the lower end of manropes when the lanyard was spliced in back.

Plate 47. MISCELLANEOUS KNOTWORK

Fig. 229—A CIRCULAR NET which is often called a shot or treasure net. To begin, fill the meshing needle with line of the required size. Stretch the headrope in circular fashion and start on the left side by securing the line with a clove hitch to the headrope. The meshes are formed in the usual way, and the circumference of the net is reduced as the work continues down toward the end, by bringing two meshes into one at regular intervals. At first one mesh in a row is brought

113

in, then in the next row two meshes. Next, take up every fourth mesh, and then every third in a row, and so on. Work a small grommet through the meshes at the bottom to hold them together. Reeve two straps through the head to be used as beckets for hauling apart, in order to draw the mouth of the net up.

Fig. 230—A NEEDLE HITCHED ROPE POINTING such as this is worked in the same general way as fender hitching, which is of similar principle, except that it is worked down into a tapered, cone-shaped point on the end of a rope that has already been prepared by scraping the yarns until they are thinned down enough to assume a tapered or pointed effect. The first five or six turns are snaked in the manner illustrated. Pointing a rope in this manner is considered more practical than the early style of pointing a rope with its own yarns, which is now an obsolete practice.

Fig. 231—WORMING, PARCELING, and SERVING. These are the three essential types of work necessary to protect a rope from chafing or from rotting, due to dampness.

Worming consists of laying strands of marline, spun yarn, or other suitable material along the spiral grooves of the rope, in the direction of the lay of the rope. This is done to fill in the hollow grooves in the rope and to give it a smooth, round appearance.

Parceling consists of small strips of canvas, usually tarred, which are wrapped around the rope, with the lay, by overlapping one turn over the other. This is done to give the overlapping turns a tendency to shed water.

Serving consists of a tight binding of marline or spun yarn around and against the lay of the rope, which has previously been wormed and parceled. This work is done with a serving mallet and two men are necessary to do the work. The marline is wrapped around the handle of the serving mallet, as illustrated. It is then passed around the rope, two or three turns being made, depending upon how tight the service is to be. The mallet is passed around the rope, with each revolution adding an additional turn to the service. Remember the old adage:

Worm and parcel with the lay;
Turn and serve the other way.

Fig. 232—An ARCTIC WHALING IRON of this type is a relic of the past. A whale line was bent or made fast to the harpoon becket by means of a double becket hitch, Plate 29, Fig. 110. In reality, both this and the following diagram were much longer in actual size, but these examples are presented in limited space and are shown only as replicas of a forgotten past.

Fig. 233—A SPERM-WHALE IRON is shown here as it was mounted for use.

Fig. 234—The WROUGHT or PAUNCH MAT is begun by taking any desired number of strands and middling them over a lashing. Next, bring the underneath strand over the top strand of each set, from right to left, all the way across. Pass each strand under two strands toward the right side, and back over the same two strands toward the left side. Follow this procedure with each strand in turn, until the weave reaches the required length. The outside strand on each side serves as a filler for attaching the other strands. In this method, it will be noted that the strands are worked down into a point on the left side by tapering the weave from the right side down. This is one of the early type of mats once used for heavy rigging on sailing ships. It also makes an attractive design for covering sennit frames.

Fig. 235A—The NAPOLEON BEND or OCEAN PLAT MAT WEAVE may be tied by using several methods, such as beginning with the pulled-out bight of an overhand knot, etc., but the method of forming the pattern of the weave, as presented here, is somewhat different in this instance, as can be readily noted from the formation of the partly completed design.

Fig. 235B—With the weave closed up, as indicated by the drawn-in lines in the last diagram, the weave will assume this appearance when it has all its parts doubled. This type of weave makes an attractive ornamental decoration and is often used as a floor mat when woven with Manila rope.

Plate 48. EMERGENCY FISHHOOK TIES, WHALING IRONS, ETC.

Fig. 236—A LATCH BARB HOOK such as this represents one of many different ways of constructing an emergency fishhook

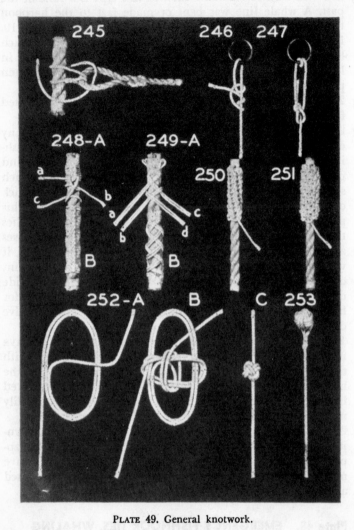

PLATE 49. General knotwork.

when nothing but crude material for such purposes is available. When castaways are lost or stranded in remote parts of the world, there is always a much better chance to survive along a body of water. Edible foods are generally more abundant in water than on land. Fish feed at all times of the day and night, depending upon their species and certain other factors that govern their feeding activities, such as the type of food that is available in their locality at any time of the year, which is largely influenced by seasonal changes, but in general, early morning and late afternoon are usually the best periods of time to fish when using bait.

Fig. 237—A WOODEN SHAFTED HOOK with wood barb makes a suitable emergency tie that can be made with very little effort. Any kind of twine, or even small strips of bark, may be used as seizings on this type of hook.

Fig. 238—A WOODEN SHAFTED HOOK with a fish spine barb.

Fig. 239—A WOODEN SHAFTED HOOK such as this may be constructed by using a shoe nail or a stiff thorn for a barb.

Fig. 240—A FISH SPEAR TRAP. The trigger stick is released when a fish is speared, thus causing the barbs to clamp tight and hold the fish in a viselike grip. It may be fashioned from wood or bamboo, in the manner illustrated.

Fig. 241—HOW TO PREVENT AN ANCHOR FROM FOULING. For still fish and fly casting have about one hundred or more feet of light rope attached to an anchor rigged like the one shown here, which cannot get stuck under a rock. If the wind blows inshore, anchor off the shore, the ledge or the hole toward which you are fishing; you will find that by letting out more rope you will drift inshore toward your ledge or hole and can fish various depths without taking up anchor. Reverse the process if wind is blowing offshore, etc.

To get greater efficiency while still fishing, take two anchors, one at each end of your long rope. With each anchor out you can then silently move your boat along the rope, changing depths and places you fish in without disturbing the fish. Moreover, your boat, anchored at both ends, will not sway with the wind and frighten the fish.

When fishing from a boat, never drop your anchor over the spot where you intend to fish, as this has a tendency to frighten the fish away. Lower it quietly some distance away and either drift or paddle to the proper location.

To prevent loss of anchors by fouling, the rope is hitched to where the shaft joins the curved flukes, then attached to the outside of the ring with a turn or two of fishing line. An anchor thus attached is used in the ordinary manner, but if it should become snagged, a hard pull will break the fishing line and allow the flukes to be unhooked very easily by the backward pull of the line on them.

Fig. 242—A TWO-FLUED ARCTIC WHALING IRON with harpoon mounting and ringbolt hitching, such as this, represents a relic of the bygone whaling days of the seventeenth and eighteenth centuries. This and the two following irons were much longer than illustrated here, as limited space would not permit longer diagrams. The two-flued iron went out of use in the whaling industry prior to 1850.

Fig. 243—A TOGGLE IRON with ringbolt hitching such as this has a spliced eye around its socket.

Fig. 244—A ONE-FLUED IRON such as this had grafted mounting. It likewise went out of use more than a century ago.

Plate 49. GENERAL KNOTWORK

Fig. 245—The proper way to RATTLE DOWN, i.e., secure a ratline to a shroud, is shown in the accompanying illustration. The eyes spliced into the ends of the ratlines are made fast to the shrouds by lashings. These are passed through the eyes, as illustrated, and after a sufficient number of turns have been taken with the lashing, several cross turns are taken and the ends are secured with a clove hitch. It will be noticed in this connection that the eyes spliced in the ratlines are always secured to the shrouds with the flat surface of the eye facing upward. This eliminates the possibility of rain water lying in the cup on the bottom of the eye.

Fig. 246—The MIDSHIPMAN'S HITCH shown here is a variation of the standard method of forming this knot, as illustrated in Plate 16, Fig. 14. By forming the tie in a slightly different manner, with the working end reversed to come out on the side opposite to that in the former method, the knot is less likely to capsize under a strain, thereby making this tie more dependable.

Fig. 247—The ANCHOR BOWLINE represents one of the common methods of bending an anchor line to an anchor ring.

Figs. 248A and B—The COMMON THREE-STRAND COXCOMB is tied as follows: Seize three strands to a rail or other object; next, take one strand and form a left-handed half hitch. With another strand, form a right-handed half hitch. Then tie a left-handed half hitch. In the illustration, *a* has been half-hitched to the left, *b* to the right, and *c* to the left. The next step is to begin with *a* again, hitching it to the right this time. The complete coxcomb is shown in Fig. 248B.

Figs. 249A and B—The FOUR-STRAND COACH WHIPPING or CROSS-POINTING is tied by the same method as a round sennit braid. In addition to its use as a braided line, it can also be formed around a core, as a covering for a stanchion, telescope, rope point, etc. It can be made with any even number of strands, which are often doubled, trebled or quadrupled. To begin, take strand *c* and lay it across strand *a*. Strand *b* is brought around over *c* and under *d,* toward the opposite side. Follow up by bringing strand *a* around under *c* and over *d* to its own side. Then bring strand *c* around under *b* and over *a* to its own side, and so on, until the desired number of passes has been made. Fig. 249A shows how the seizings are made to start, and Fig. 249B shows the coach whipping completed.

Fig. 250—The OPEN FENDER HITCHING is the method of hitching used to cover large fenders, such as those on the bow of a tugboat—a familiar sight to everyone. This type of hitching is done with one strand. To begin, take two complete turns around the work with the end of the strand. Take the other end and begin half-hitching on these two turns until you have gone completely around the fender or rope. The next half hitch is taken on the bight, between two of the first group of half hitches that has been made. This is continued until the desired length is reached. It will be found necessary, when covering a large fender, to add a length of line from time to time; this can be accomplished by long-splicing the two ends together. When working on an irregular surface, a half hitch can be left out or can be added at intervals, whichever may be necessary.

Fig. 251—The CLOSED FENDER HITCHING is made in the same way

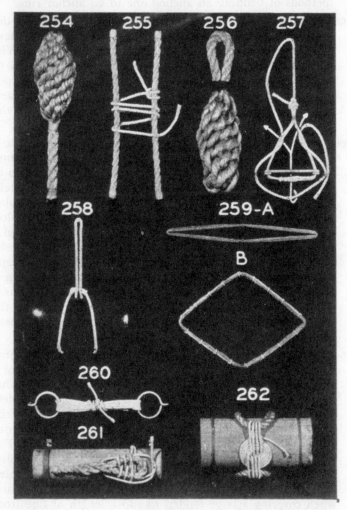

PLATE 50. Boatswain's chair and lashings.

as the hitching in Fig. 250. The hitches are taken much closer together, however, so that the core upon which the work is being done can barely be seen through the hitching, and the form of hitching is inverted or opposite from the preceding method.

Figs. 252A, B and C—The MONKEY FIST is a type of knot used to put weight on the end of a heaving line. To make it, form two or three loops (usually three). Two are used here for the sake of clarity in the illustration. After forming the two loops as shown in Fig. 252A, pass the end around the first set of loops; take two more turns, and pass the end through the first set of loops and around the second set of loops, as shown in Fig. 252B. Then take two more turns, as before, and pull up taut. Care should be taken in working this knot up taut, in order to get the proper shape. Fig. 252C shows the knot as it looks when pulled up.

Fig. 253—The THREE-STRAND MONKEY FIST is the regular form of monkey fist used for heaving lines. It is made by taking three turns instead of two, but is otherwise tied in the same way as in Fig. 252.

Plate 50.   BOATSWAIN'S CHAIR AND LASHINGS

Fig. 254—The CROWNED MONKEY FIST has a series of spiral crowns worked around a core and then finished off with a spritsail sheet weave on top, which is nothing more than bringing one outside strand from each side toward the opposite side or, in other words, laying them parallel to each other but leading in opposite directions. The side strands are then alternately tucked over and under the cross strands in order to close the weave up.

Fig. 255—TRICING IN TWO ROPES is done in the following manner: A short piece of line is made fast to one of the two ropes and then several turns are taken around both of them, as illustrated. Pull all of the slack out of the two ropes by hauling on the free end of the lashing, and then secure one end of the latter to either of the ropes with a clove hitch.

Fig. 256—A SPIRAL FENDER, 16 inches in length and 2½ inches in diameter, requires 3 fathoms of ¾-inch rope. It is made in the following manner: The first step is to middle the rope and then clap on a stout seizing to form a small eye. Next,

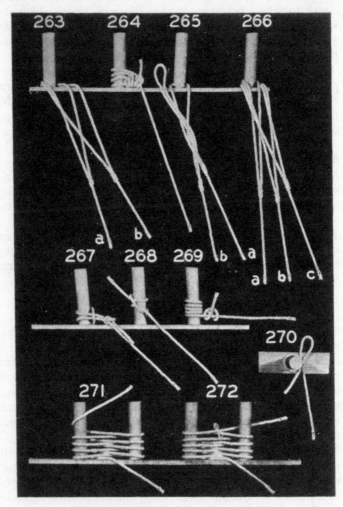

PLATE 51. Method of securing hawsers.

unlay all the strands and whip the end of each. Take the strands and form a continuous series of crowns in one direction; continue these crowns until the fender is about 18 inches in length. Do not pull the crowns up taut, but as they are made, merely take out the slack. Next, pass a stout piece of twine up through the center of the fender. All of the six strands of the rope are then attached to this piece of twine and are pulled up inside the crowns, after which each one of the strands is pulled out separately through the six openings just below the seizing. Then, with the use of a fid, proceed to draw the slack out of the crowns until the entire fender has been drawn up as taut as possible. Pull the ends of the strands out until they are drawn up tautly and cut them off short below the seizing. The method shown here is finished off with a spritsail sheet weave for convenience of presentation.

Fig. 257—RIGGING FOR A BOATSWAIN'S CHAIR is shown in the accompanying illustration. After the gantline has been rove through the block and secured to the chair bridle, as shown, and the workman has been hauled up, he places the hauling part of the rope in front of him, grasps a bight and draws it through the bridle. The line is then passed over the workman's head and body, down under the chair and up in front of him again, as shown by the arrow. All of the slack is hauled out of the line and it is then secured. To lower the chair, all that is necessary is to slack off on the knot and allow the line to run out.

Fig. 258—The BALE SLING shows the proper method of passing a strop on a bale or sack.

Figs. 259A and B—The SELVAGE STROP is stronger than a spliced strop of the same number of yarns. It is usually made of small line (marline, rope yarn, spun yarn) or of rope, warped around two spikes which are spaced the desired distance apart. When enough turns have been made, the ends are square-knotted together and temporary seizings placed on the strop. Its entire length is then lashed with marline hitching.

Fig. 260—A WEDDING LASHING is used to join the two eyes which have been previously made in the ends of two ropes. The lashing line is passed successively through the eyes a number

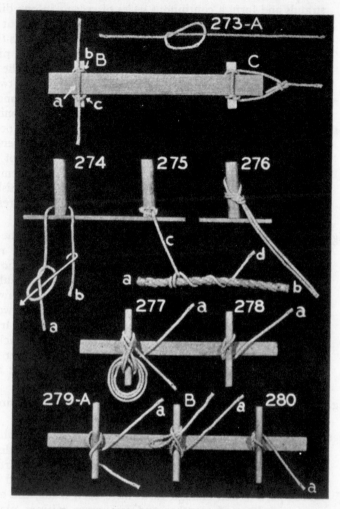

PLATE 52. A stage sling and belaying pin ties.

of times, after which the ends of the lashing are passed down between the turns and additional turns are taken over the body of the lashing, the ends of the lashing line being passed in opposite directions. The ends are finally secured with a square knot in the center, as shown.

Fig. 261—The ROSE LASHING shown here was used on sailing ships to lash the footropes to the yards. It can also be used to lash an eye to a spar, as illustrated. The method of tying the knot is self-explanatory.

Fig. 262—Another form of ROSE LASHING. It is used to secure a rope, with eyes spliced into each end, around a mast or spar. A lanyard is spliced through one eye and then passed in figure-of-eight fashion over and back under one eye, then over and back under the other. This process is continued until a sufficient number of turns have been made. The end is then taken around and around in coil fashion between the cross turns, as shown.

Plate 51. METHOD OF SECURING HAWSERS

Fig. 263—PLACING HAWSERS OVER A BOLLARD on a dock should be done in such a manner that no matter how many hawsers are used, each can be removed or cast off without interfering with the others. This is done in the following manner: Assume that the bight of the hawser marked *b* was placed over the bollard first, then, when the second hawser *a* is passed, its bight is brought up through the bight of hawser *b*, as illustrated. If the bight of hawser *a* were not brought up through that of *b*, it would not be possible to cast off hawser *b* without first releasing hawser *a*, which would not in all cases be desirable.

Fig. 264—The SINGLE CHAIN FASTENING is used over a single pile in the water. It consists of a series of figure-of-eight turns taken around the pile and over the standing part of the line, after which the end is secured with two half hitches.

Fig. 265—SECURING A HAWSER ON A BOLLARD with a round turn. It occasionally happens that when a hawser is passed over a bollard, it is given a round turn, such as is indicated with the hawser *a* in the accompanying illustration. When this is the case, the hawser would not run free when cast off, as it would in the case shown in Fig. 263. To prevent such an occurrence, the bight of the second hawser *b* is rove through the bight of hawser *a,* as shown, before being put over the pile. Either of the two hawsers can then be cast off without interfering with the other.

Fig. 266—THREE HAWSERS ON ONE BOLLARD. It is sometimes necessary to pass three or more hawsers over the same bollard. If this is done, the bight of each line (*a, b* and *c*) must pass up through the eyes of all of the others, as shown in the illustration. By performing the operation in this manner, any single line may be cast free.

Fig. 267—The LARK'S HEAD MOORING HITCH is another simple method for securing a mooring line to a pile.

Fig. 268—The CLOVE HITCH MOORING is used for the same purpose as that in the example above.

Fig. 269—The ROUND TURN MOORING HITCH is made by passing several turns around a pile, after which the end is made secure with two half hitches.

Fig. 270—The SLIPPERY HITCH is a knot that should always be used on the sheets of small sailboats. One pull on the end will release the sheet. This is often desirable when a sudden puff of wind hits the sail and there is danger that the boat might capsize.

Fig. 271—SECURING A MOORING LINE, first method. This is a means of securing a mooring line with a series of figure-of-eight turns about a pair of bitts. The end of the line may be half-hitched to one of the bitts or it may be seized as shown in Fig. 272.

Fig. 272—SECURING A MOORING LINE, second method. This illustration is the same as Fig. 271, except that the end of the line is shown seized to prevent its running out. A seizing such as this is always applied when wire rope is used.

Plate 52.   A STAGE SLING AND BELAYING PIN TIES

Fig. 273A—The STAGE SLING is a rope design often found very useful by sailors. When working over the side of a ship or in a shipyard, it is frequently found necessary to have a light yet sturdy scaffold capable of supporting one or two men. This need can be served by what is known as a stage, consisting

126

of a long flat plank with two "horns" bolted at right angles to the plank. The purpose of these horns is to keep the plank away from the surface being worked on. In order to suspend the stage from—let us say—a ship's side, it must be rigged with ropes. This is done as follows: First, lay out the rope, as shown, into a marlinespike hitch. This is made a short distance from the end.

Fig. 273B—Next, place the knot under the horn, bring part *a* over the top of the stage. Bights *b* and *c* are then brought over and on top of the horns on each side.

Fig. 273C—The end is now brought up and a bowline formed, using the end and the standing part, as indicated. But, before drawing the knot taut, be certain that both parts are even, so that the stage will not be canted when it hangs on the rope. One of these knots is made on each horn. The standing parts may be rove through the blocks on the deck above, with the ends brought down and made fast to the stage. This eliminates climbing back up on deck to lower the stage—which would be necessary if it were made fast to a railing.

Fig. 274—The HEAVING LINE BOWLINE is another knot of great usefulness to seafaring men. When docking a ship and sending the hawsers ashore, the operation must, as a rule, be carried out as quickly as possible. After the heaving line has been cast ashore, there is usually a good deal of unnecessary fumbling in making the end fast to the eye of the hawser. This can be eliminated by tying a bowline, using the method illustrated here. The end of the line is first rove through the eye of the hawser. Then take the standing part of line *a* in the left hand and place it in the position shown. End *b*, which is in the right hand, is next passed under the middle strand, as shown by the arrow. Now cast end *b* away from you, and at the same time give standing part *a* a sharp jerk. The knot will automatically fall into a bowline. Although this method appears to be a bit drawn out, a little practice will enable anyone to tie the knot in half the time required to tie a bowline in the ordinary manner. This method can be used also when making fast to a pile (as in the illustration), or in any other situation where a bowline is advisable.

Fig. 275—The STOPPER may be applied when tying up a ship, or

127

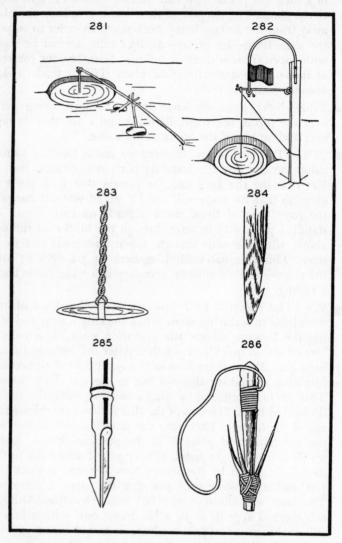

PLATE 53. Fishing through the ice, a grapple, spears, etc.

when a heavy load is to be suspended and it is desired to take the rope off the niggerhead or capstan. End *a* is the part leading to the capstan, and standing part *b* leads to the load. The stopper, *c,* is made fast to the bitts and secured to the working line with a stopper hitch, the end being "dogged" with the lay, and the bitter end, *d,* held in the hand. End *a* is next slacked off the capstan until the stopper is bearing all the strain. Then make end *a* fast to the bitts or chock, whichever is used, and remove the stopper to complete the operation.

Fig. 276—The OVERHAND WHARF TIE is an easy method of making a line fast to a pile on a dock when only the bight of the line is available. A simple overhand knot is first made in such a way that when the operation has been completed the bight will face upward. All that then remains is to cast the bight over the top of the pile.

Fig. 277—COILING ROPE ON A BELAYING PIN. This is the correct method for coiling the end of a rope on a belaying pin. When a considerable amount of rope remains left over after the rope has been belayed, the remainder is then coiled up in the hand and, when near the end, the coil is placed against the pinrail and several more turns are taken on the belaying pin. This uses up the remaining end and also secures the coil, as illustrated; *a* is the standing part.

Fig. 278—The correct method of BELAYING AN EYE-SPLICED LINE. When the standing part of the rope leads from above, the end is brought around in back of the belaying pin, beneath the pinrail, and then the eye is placed over the top of the belaying pin.

Figs. 279A and B—BELAYING A LINE TO A BELAYING PIN is done as shown. The rope is first brought around the pin, then up and around the top of it, after which a number of figure-of-eight turns are taken around the line and the pin; *a* represents the standing part. When enough turns have been taken, the end is finished off with a slippery hitch, as illustrated in Fig. 279B.

Fig. 280—Another method of MAKING AN EYE FAST TO A BELAYING PIN. When the standing part, *a,* leads from below, the end is first brought around the top of the belaying pin, and the eye is passed over the bottom of the pin to finish.

Plate 53. FISHING THROUGH THE ICE, A GRAPPLE,
SPEARS, ETC.

Fig. 281—ICE FISHING may be accomplished by using various
methods to rig devices with which to fish. The diagram
shown here represents a very simple and easy way to rig a
pole. An ax will be necessary to cut holes in the ice when
it is thick and frozen hard. A hole is usually chopped about
10 to 12 inches in diameter, but take care not to chop all
the way through the ice. When within several inches of the
bottom of the ice, a long-handled chisel can best be used to
flare it out, as an ax, if used for this purpose, would wet the
user with splashing water which would freeze. Before using
a chisel in the bottom of an ice hole, be sure to have a piece
of cord attached to it and secure it around your waist or to
your belt. This will prevent losing the chisel. A hole can be
drilled in the handle of the chisel with which to fasten the
cord.

Pickerel are usually found in deep water near beds of weeds
and lilies. It is best to keep chopping holes in the ice until
the right location is found, as these fish lurk in or near such
places the greater part of the winter.

From 20 to 30 feet of linen line about 18- or 20-lb. test will
be sufficient for ice fishing in most cases. The most satisfactory bait for such a purpose is live minnows. When fishing
for any length of time from an ice hole in winter, a dipper
of some sort is required to remove slush from the bottom to
prevent it from freezing over again and closing the hole.

The most popular form of ice fishing is that which is known
as a tipup arrangement. This includes a pole which is used
for a crosspiece. It should be long enough to reach from one
side of the ice hole to the other, when placed across the center. Another pole is then lashed crosswise to this support,
leaving enough length on the end of the pole to secure the
fishline, and so that it will tip properly when a fish is caught.
The opposite end should extend out over the edge of the
hole. A piece of colored cloth is attached to this end, which
serves as a flag or an automatic signaling device on the tipup
pole when there is a fish on the line, which automatically
brings the flag to an upright position.

Fig. 282—This represents another practical and somewhat more precise arrangement for ice fishing, which was used by the authors in Canada many years ago with satisfactory results. The illustration is self-explanatory, but the following words will help simplify its construction. Any kind of board can be used for the upright support. It should be about 1½ feet long and 1½ to 2 inches broad. This serves as the tipup foundation. A small hole near the ice hole will be necessary to anchor this object in. Other materials which are required include a piece of heavy wire about 8 or 10 inches long to be used as a trigger, which has an eye formed on each end, as illustrated, with enough end left extending out to hold the fishline, as indicated at *a*. It is fastened with a staple through its eye about 6 inches from the top of the upright support. Attach a spring to the upright with staples.

A piece of cloth which serves as a flag is then secured to the opposite end of the spring. Leave enough space below the flag on the end of the spring so that it can be inserted through the eye of the trigger, as indicated at *b*. The amount of fishline to use in a case of this sort can best be determined by sounding the depth of the water before deciding on the proper length of line. After the spring has been pulled down, with the trigger "set" by inserting the end of the spring through the eye of the trigger, there will be enough tension to hold the trigger in a horizontal position.

Fig. 283—A GORGE, such as that shown here, represents the earliest known type of fishhook. Among the inhabitants of the old Stone Age, man had already begun to fashion these crude implements with which to catch fish.

Fig. 284—A FISH SPEAR such as this may be fashioned from wood, a heavy thorn, or any number of things. This is an excellent way to kill large fish in waters where they are numerous.

Fig. 285—A FISH SPEAR of this type may be made from hollow bamboo, in the manner illustrated.

Fig. 286—A BAIT GRAPPLE which can be used for hauling in small forms of drifting sea life from salt-water depths. This form of life makes excellent bait, as it serves as food for most larger forms of aquatic life. It may be constructed with the use of thorns for grapples, which are bound to a heavy wooden shaft, as indicated.

CHAPTER III

Fishing Traps and Seines

SINCE no book dealing with fishermen's knots would be complete without an adequate coverage of the various types of practical fishing traps and seines, we have endeavored to include in this chapter all of the more commonly known and widely used methods in this field. There are numerous examples presented here that are familiar to fishermen wherever fish are caught. Gill, trammel, pound, hoop, fyke and trap nets are numbered among this interesting variety, which comes under the general heading of fishing traps.

An ample explanation of the various uses to which they are put, and complete instructions as to how they are constructed, will provide valuable information for everyone who has a desire to become acquainted with this particular field of fishing, whether it be merely from the standpoint of an amateur or for the practical use of the more experienced commercial fisherman.

Straight and tapered seines are also dealt with, and special rules for finding the length of tie spaces when hanging nets are likewise included.

Plate 54. TUNNEL, FYKE AND GILL NETS

Fig. 1—A TUNNEL or HOOP NET. Nets such as this are used as traps and are very effective in rivers and other waters where fish "run" in some general direction. The fish work through the throats or tunnels and are unable to find their way out again. Bait is sometimes attached inside these nets to attract fish.

Fig. 2—A FYKE NET with wings. Wings for nets such as this are hung on rope, with floats and leads attached. The hoops that are used are usually of a fine quality of oak.

Fig. 3—A GILL or SET NET. Gill nets are usually set on the bottom and stretched out as tight as possible, the ends being

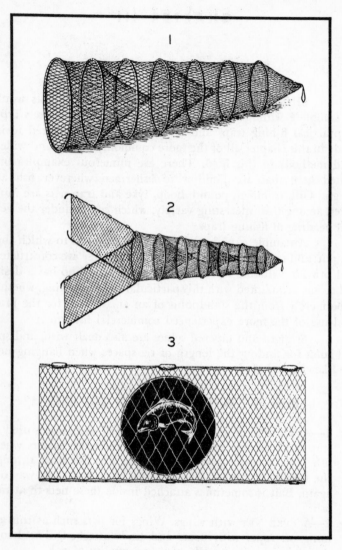

PLATE 54. Tunnel, fyke and gill nets.

secured by some kind of anchorage. They are made of strong, fine thread, and fish striking them pass their heads through the mesh and are caught behind the gills. Proper fullness of webbing is important in nets of this kind, as too much or too little web may affect their wearing quality as well as the way they fish.

Plate 55. A TRAMMEL NET AND SEINES

Fig. 4—A TRAMMEL NET. Trammel nets are made up of three sheets of netting: One web of small mesh usually of linen twine is hung between two outer webs or "walls" of large mesh cotton. The net is set taut across a stream, and fish striking it push the fine inside netting through the larger meshes of the "walls" and thus pocket themselves.

Fig. 5—A STRAIGHT SEINE. This is probably the oldest type of fish net which is known. In its simplest form, it may be a little one-man minnow net pushed ahead of the fisherman with a pair of stakes. In its commercial form, it may be hundreds of yards long, requiring a powerful ship—a "dragger" —to encircle the school of fish. Both straight and tapered seines, as illustrated on this plate, are usually hung on a one-third basis, which means using 18 inches of netting "stretched" to 12 inches of rope. The top line is single and the bottom line is doubled and of opposite twist or lay to prevent the seine from rolling. Straight seines are usually ordered by the fisherman to suit his own ideas, and he specifies the depth in number of meshes, size of mesh, and basis or fullness in hanging. Straight seines are most generally made up in soft-laid twine.

Fig. 6—A TAPERED SEINE.

Plate 56. RULES FOR GILL NETS, MESH MEASUREMENTS AND HANGING NETS

Figs. 7 and 8—GILL NET RULES which are self-explanatory.

Fig. 9—When making or ordering nets, the proper depth, size of mesh and size of twine must first be determined. In seines, the size of top and bottom lines, size and type of floats, whether cedar or cork, and also the proper size of leads, and

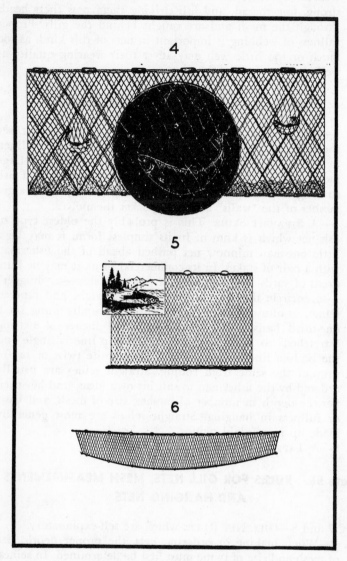

PLATE 55. A trammel net and seines.

how far apart floats and leads are to be placed, must likewise be predetermined. Dimensions must also include proper specifications when speaking of mesh sizes, such as to whether the correct understanding of hanging or stretched mesh is properly applied in advance calculations. This is usually referred to as stretched or square measure, such as the case may be. Ordinarily, for seines one third is allowed, or in other words, netting intended to hang 100 feet by 10 feet would require 150 feet by 15 feet stretched measure. It is also convenient to calculate the depth of meshes before proceeding on an undertaking of this kind. The lower diagram illustrates the rule for measuring stretched mesh.

Fig. 10—To find the length of tie space when hanging nets, draw two vertical lines 12 inches apart, *a* and *b* in diagram. Next draw a third line, *c,* diagonally from *a* to *b,* making the length of this line equal to your basis figure. For instance, if you are hanging netting 19 inches to the foot, make line *c* nineteen inches long. Then, starting at the lower end, mark off on *c* spaces equal to the intended size of mesh. Count off the number of meshes you are picking up to the tie—for instance, 3—and measure the distance from the end of the third space to line *a*. This will give you the length of tie for 3 meshes on the basis of 19 inches to the foot. If your basis is 20 inches to the foot, make line *c* 20 inches long, and follow this same rule with any basis you wish to figure.

APPROXIMATE YARDAGE OF MEDIUM SEINE TWINE

Size	Feet Per Lb.	Size	Feet Per Lb.
6	3300	48	390
9	2000	54	345
12	1650	60	270
15	1320	72	220
18	1100	84	190
21	890	96	170
24	830	108	150
27	690	120	130
30	620	132	120
36	520	138	115
42	445	144	110

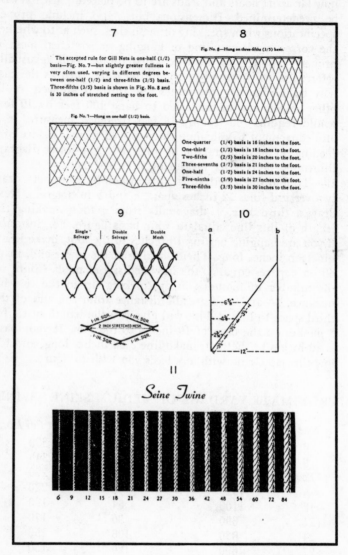

7

The accepted rule for Gill Nets is one-half (1/2) basis—Fig. No. 7—but slightly greater fullness is very often used, varying in different degrees between one-half (1/2) and three-fifths (3/5) basis. Three-fifths (3/5) basis is shown in Fig. No. 8 and is 30 inches of stretched netting to the foot.

Fig. No. 7—Hung on one-half (1/2) basis.

8

Fig. No. 8—Hung on three-fifths (3/5) basis.

One-quarter	(1/4)	basis is 16 inches to the foot.
One-third	(1/3)	basis is 18 inches to the foot.
Two-fifths	(2/5)	basis is 20 inches to the foot.
Three-sevenths	(3/7)	basis is 21 inches to the foot.
One-half	(1/2)	basis is 24 inches to the foot.
Five-ninths	(5/9)	basis is 27 inches to the foot.
Three-fifths	(3/5)	basis is 30 inches to the foot.

9

Single Selvage | Double Selvage | Double Mesh

1-IN. SQR.   1-IN. SQR.
2 INCH STRETCHED MESH
1-IN. SQR.   1-IN. SQR.

10

a   b

c

6 5/8"
4 1/2"
3 3/8"
2 1/4"
12"

11

Seine Twine

6 9 12 15 18 21 24 27 30 36 42 48 54 60 72 84

PLATE 56. Rules for gill nets, mesh measurements and hanging nets.

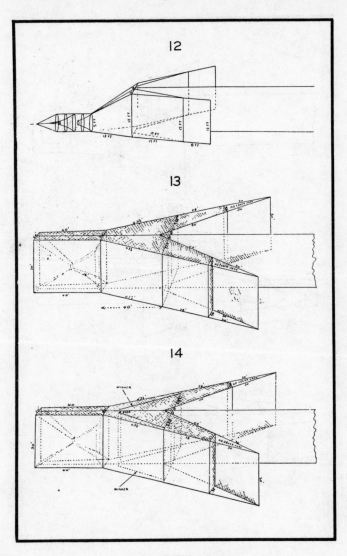

PLATE 57. Trap nets.

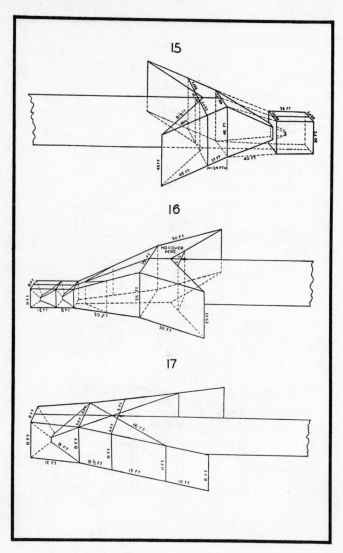

PLATE 58. Trap nets.

Fig. 11—This shows the different sizes of Ederer seine twine, which is generally used in the best grade nets.

Plate 57.   TRAP NETS

Fig. 12—A Hoop Net Trap. Traps with hoop net pots are used in a number of localities and seem to be quite successful. Some fishermen want the slope or long tunnel straight on the bottom, but others prefer them tapered, top and bottom, so that the pot sets in the middle of the water. In these pots, special care should be used in the construction of the throats, as "old timers" say that this is the most important part of the net.

Fig. 13—A Trap Net with short tunnel. The short tunnel design offers a slight saving in cost of construction over the older, long tunnel type, and reports regarding its efficiency are very favorable. The elimination of the long tunnel, besides reducing the cost of production, makes the net easier to handle, which is a good point in its favor; and it also requires fewer anchors than the larger net. The diagram illustrates a net with webbing running only part way to the points of the hearts. This feature is not essential, but the idea is to save material and also to eliminate the sharp angle of the point in which fish are often entangled.

Fig. 14—A Trap Net with short tunnel and winkers. The net illustrated here adopts the idea, used largely on Lake Erie, of "winkers" or inner hearts. These winkers can be added to the net with very little extra effort or cost, and they are effective in offering an additional barrier to the escape of the fish. The position of the winkers varies in different localities and according to the ideas of the fishermen. Some start them midway between the pot and breast, instead of right at the breast, as shown here.

Plate 58.   TRAP NETS

Fig. 15—A Deep-Water Trap. A net such as this is more commonly known as a submarine trap net. This type of net is similar in construction and dimensions to pound nets, but

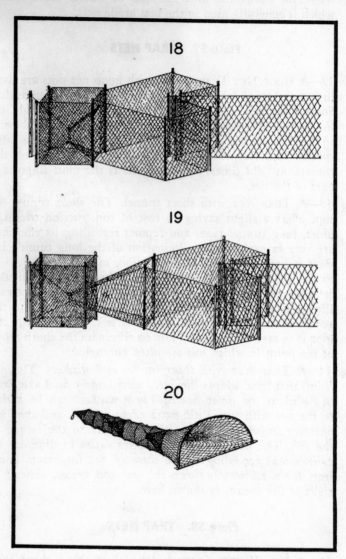

PLATE 59. Pound and hoop nets.

has the advantage of being set without stakes.

Fig. 16—A LAKE ERIE TRAP. Nets of this general description are quite extensively used. They are not intended for extremely deep water, but are sometimes 30 to 35 feet deep at the heart. The pot is usually 8 or 10 feet deep. There are no covers at top and bottom of the hearts, this part being open. They are set without stakes, and are held in place with anchors, buoys, weights, etc.

Fig. 17—A SUBMARINE TRAP. These nets are used in many localities. They are built in various ways and in a variety of dimensions, but this diagram gives a general idea of their construction. A depth of 8 feet seems to be about the average. Some fishermen prefer tapered pots so that the outside edges will form approximately a straight line with the rest of the net—others want the pots straight. This diagram shows the inner heart only 8½ feet long, but they are often longer. These nets have the advantage of being comparatively inexpensive to build.

Plate 59.   POUND AND HOOP NETS

Fig. 18—A SHORT TUNNEL POUND NET. Pound nets are very widely used, and all commercial fishermen are familiar with them. However, in some localities men are not acquainted with the long tunnel type, while in other places the short tunnel type is a stranger. It is generally agreed that the construction of the tunnel is the most important part in building these nets. It must be just right so that the fish will find their way easily into the pot, without a loose, flopping web to scare them back or dark spots to appear like obstructions to them.

The ropes on the gores must be the proper length, the webbing should have the right fullness so that it will hang taut but not too taut, and the slope of the top and bottom should be at the proper angle. Many fishermen find it desirable to have the throat of the tunnel set close to the bottom, claiming that the fish do not climb readily if the angle is too sharp. This is particularly true in long tunnel nets, but may also apply to the short tunnel type. On the other hand, if it is known that the fish are not swimming close to the bottom, it is desirable to have the throat set higher. These are points for fishermen to determine according to their own conditions and experience. The great majority of pound nets are constructed with the web hung on "1/3 basis," but many fishermen find it an advantage to use slightly more fullness in the length of the web, say about 20 inches to the foot, to allow for shrinkage, etc. This adds little to the cost of construction, but lengthens the life of the web because there is less strain.

Fig. 19—A Long Tunnel Pound Net.

Fig. 20—A Brook Hoop Net. This type of net is very effective for small fish and should come in handy for trapping brook chubs for live bait.

CHAPTER IV

Netmaking and Repairing

GENERAL information on netmaking and repairing has been of such a limited nature heretofore that those who have a desire to acquire skill along this line have found it most diffi- cult to obtain informative knowledge from any source other than commercial market fishermen, or from a few of the ever-diminish- ing number of old shellbacks who still retain their ability to perform work of this nature, which was ordinarily a customary part of their experience acquired in general knotwork and mar- linespike seamanship in years gone by.

Even though it is not anticipated that everyone reading this chapter will have the desire to make any large amount of nets, nevertheless, practice in making portions of nets is essential if one is to develop the manual skill required to make a satis- factory repair, which is likely to be necessary at almost any time on nets that are subject to average usage.

Considerable detailed instructions are included here on almost every phase of netmaking in various stages of construc- tion. Ample explanation is also given on how to mend and re- pair a torn or otherwise damaged net with patch work. The proper way to reduce and increase meshes by diminishing or adding to the number of meshes in a row, such as the case may be, is also covered.

Landing nets are likewise discussed at great length and their method of construction is elaborated upon in each stage of development.

Plate 60.   NETTING SHUTTLES OR NEEDLES

Fig. 1—Shows a standard type of shuttle that is available in the commercial market. Shuttles such as these are made of thin, hard wood $6\frac{1}{2}$ to 8 inches long and $\frac{5}{8}$ to $\frac{7}{8}$ of an inch thick.

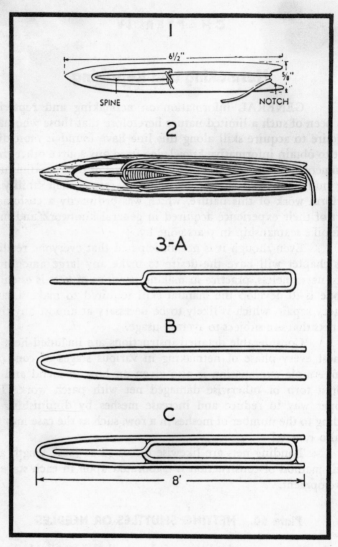

PLATE 60. Netting shuttles or needles.

Cut out the central spine just long enough so that it must be pushed to one side or the other to permit the loops of twine to pass over its point. This prevents the needle from unwinding when dropped, but permits the user to unwind one loop at a time by a slight pull toward the point of the needle.

Fig. 2—This shows a filled shuttle ready to use. To fill the shuttle, tie the end of twine around the base of the central spine with a clove hitch, as illustrated in previous diagram. Then lead the twine down one side and over the notch and up the other side to the tip of the spine. Bend the spine enough to permit the twine to loop over it and continue to wind the twine in the same way until it is approximately $1/4$ of an inch from the end of the spine. Leave a free end of about 24 inches of twine.

Fig. 3A—A good shuttle may also be made by soldering together two 15-inch lengths of 10-gauge wire after they have been bent to shape, as illustrated in the accompanying diagrams. This piece forms the body and spine. It is bent in an elongated, rectangular shape with the spine extending from the center of one end. It has a soldered joint where the end connects with the body of the wire.

Fig. 3B—This piece forms the exterior. It is bent in a simple elongated U shape.

Fig. 3C—This shows the completed shuttle after the long sides of the body have been soldered to the exterior wire. Care should be taken that the sides of the U wire extend beyond the body section.

Plate 61.   WEAVING MESHES

Fig. 4A—Make a loop by tying a bowline in the free end of the twine, as shown here.

Fig. 4B—The length of loop, when stretched so that the sides come together, should be the same as the distance between diagonally opposite knots of a mesh stretched so that the sides likewise come together. This dimension is called the "mesh." In this case, a standard camouflage net, having a $4\frac{1}{2}$ inch mesh, would have $2\frac{1}{4}$ inches on each side of the square.

147

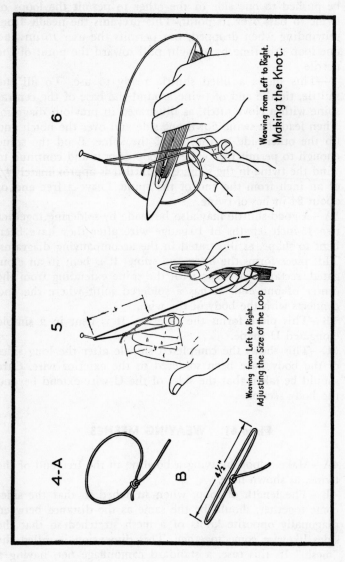

Weaving from Left to Right.
Making the Knot.

6

Weaving from Left to Right.
Adjusting the Size of the Loop.

5

4-A

B

4½"

PLATE 61. Weaving meshes.

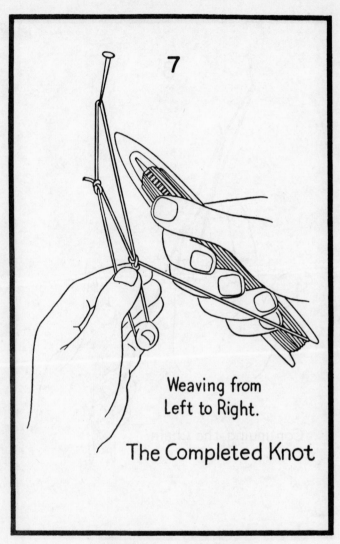

7

Weaving from
Left to Right.

The Completed Knot

PLATE 62. Mesh weaving continued.

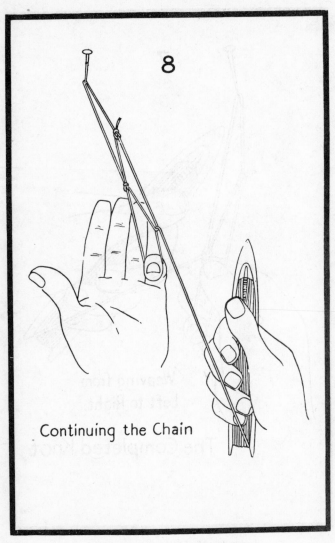

8

Continuing the Chain

PLATE 63. Lengthening the chain.

Fig. 5—The next step is to weave a chain of meshes equal to the length of the net desired. To make a chain, suspend the loop just formed from a convenient nail. Turn the loop so that the knot is in the middle of the left-hand side. Pass the shuttle up through the loop with the right hand, regrasp the shuttle with the right hand and pull it down toward the right hip. Hook the left little finger in the new loop from behind, so that loops may be grasped by the left hand. Adjust the new loop to the same size as the first one by pulling it with the shuttle or finger. Loops and twine should be stretched firmly toward the weaver at this stage.

Fig. 6—When the size of the loop is adjusted, grasp the twine where it is passed through the first loop with the left thumb and forefinger. Note that the thumb is behind the twine leading to the shuttle, and that the thumbnail grips the bottom of the first loop. Now throw a loop of twine up to the left front with the running end leading from the top of the loop. Pass the point of the shuttle behind two sides of the first loop, in front of the twine leading down from the original bowline to the left little finger, and through the loop just thrown up to the left front. Appearance of work should now be as shown.

Plate 62.   MESH WEAVING CONTINUED

Fig. 7—Regrasp the point of the shuttle with the right hand and pull the knot taut by pulling the shuttle down toward the right hip, at the same time keeping a firm hold with the left thumb and forefinger and with the left little finger. The mesh is now completed and should appear as shown. Caution: Do not release your hold with the thumb and forefinger of the left hand until the knot has been tightened.

Plate 63.   LENGTHENING THE CHAIN

Fig. 8—Remove the first loop from the nail, turn it over and replace it so that the twine again leads from the middle of the left-hand side of the loop. Weave another mesh in the same manner as the first one; turn the chain over and continue until the number of meshes desired for one side of the net have been made. After the first few meshes are woven, it is no longer necessary to remove the end loop from the nail and turn the whole chain over. The chain can be twisted until the twine leads off from the left side. After each mesh is woven, twist the chain back to weave the next mesh. If the net is to be used to patch another net, the exact number of meshes required should be counted. Otherwise, it is sufficiently close to allow 17 to $17\frac{1}{2}$ inches of chain per foot length of the edge of the net.

Plate 64. WEAVING BODY OF NET

Fig. 9—The body of the net is now made by weaving onto the side of the chain. The chain is removed from the nail and spread out, as shown. The shuttle indicates the first mesh that will be used in weaving back and forth across the net. These edge meshes may be strung on a rod. It is better to have net hang so that the loops are free to slide together, because in this way it is much easier to judge the correct size of the loop than when the loop is spread out. In either case, meshes will begin to close up after 5 or 6 rows have been woven. The hanging bar should be thrust through, as shown, so that all twine crosses the front of the bar in the same direction. This makes the net hang evenly.

Fig. 10—With the chain hung up, as shown here, the twine should lead off from the lower left-hand knot. Pass the shuttle through the mesh to the right of the knot. Hook the left little finger in the loop. Adjust the length of the loop so that the distance from the knot directly above the little finger to the bottom of the loop equals the total length of the mesh. Complete the tie in the same manner as for making the chain. Pick up the next loop to the right, tie into it, and proceed across to the right-hand edge of the net. If the chain contains an odd number of meshes, the last mesh on the right is strung on the rod (dotted lines Fig. 9) and must be skipped in weaving the body of the net.

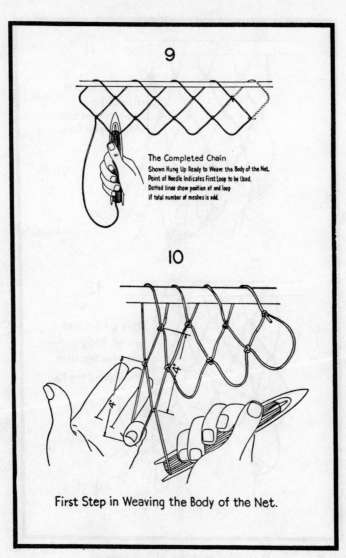

9

The Completed Chain

Shown Hung Up Ready to Weave the Body of the Net.
Point of Needle Indicates First Loop to be Used.
Dotted lines show position of end loop
if total number of meshes is odd.

10

First Step in Weaving the Body of the Net.

PLATE 64. Weaving body of net.

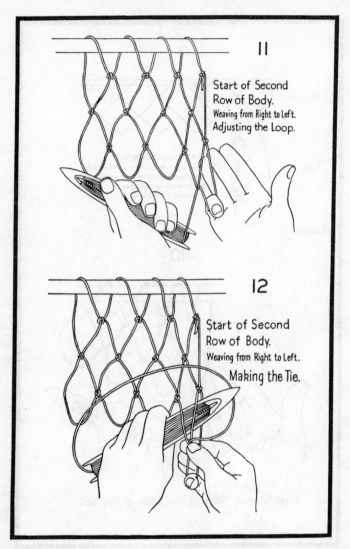

11

Start of Second
Row of Body.
Weaving from Right to Left.
Adjusting the Loop.

12

Start of Second
Row of Body.
Weaving from Right to Left.
Making the Tie.

PLATE 65. Proceeding with the weave.

Plate 65. PROCEEDING WITH THE WEAVE

Fig. 11—Change the shuttle to the left hand, pass the point up and to the front, through the last mesh woven, hook the little finger of the right hand in the loop, and adjust to the proper length, as shown here.

Fig. 12—Continue by throwing a loop of twine up to the right front, pass the shuttle from left to right behind the mesh being tied into, in front of the loop hooked on the finger, and through the loop thrown up to the right. Now pull the knot taut and continue weaving from right to left in the same manner, until the left-hand edge of the net is reached. Then change the shuttle back to the right hand and work back from left to right as in the first row of the body.

Plate 66. WEAVING CONTINUED AND TRIMMING A TEAR

Fig. 13—Continue weaving back and forth until the desired length of the net is reached. This length is determined in exactly the same manner as for a length of chain, by counting mesh as if for a patch, or measurement as if for a complete net. Ties must be made, as described, so that twine will lead directly from one knot to another without crossing the twine while coming into the knot. If trouble is experienced with twine crossing itself when ties are made as described, it indicates that the knots are not being pulled tightly into proper shape. In this case, probably the little finger is not holding the loop tightly enough as the knot is being pulled taut. If clove hitches are used to attach the work to a bar when making nets of this kind, instead of stringing or hanging the meshes on the bar, as described in this series of illustrations, the first row of loops should always be formed smaller than the subsequent rows. This is necessary because, when the clove hitches are removed from the bar on which the net was started, they will open up, thus creating a larger mesh than the others.

Fig. 14—This shows the most convenient method of cutting twine, when trimming a tear that is going to be mended.

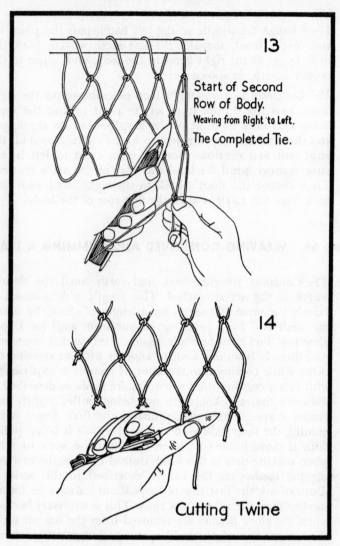

13

Start of Second
Row of Body.
Weaving from Right to Left.
The Completed Tie.

14

Cutting Twine

PLATE 66. Weaving continued and trimming a tear.

174

Plate 67. FORMATION OF A MESHING KNOT

Fig. 15A—Shows the first stage in the formation of the common sheet bend that is used in making meshes. The shuttle is put through the loop with hands in this position.

Fig. 15B—After completing the second stage of the operation, with the shuttle being pulled through underneath the loop, then down at an angle, the work will appear as shown here.

Fig. 15C—The third stage of the operation is reached with the hands and shuttle in this position.

Fig. 15D—The knot is now complete, with the line being pulled taut to bring it up in its proper place. More detailed illustrations are shown on Plates 61 and 62, Figs. 4 to 7.

Plate 68. NET REPAIRING

Fig. 16A—The first step in mending a torn or cut net, such as illustrated here, is to trim away the edges of the tear so that weaving is not interrupted by frequent cutting. This shows a section of torn net, with dotted line indicating tears.

Fig. 16B—This shows the same diagram after the two tears have been properly trimmed.

Fig. 16C—The tears are repaired by starting at Fig. 1, and then tying at Figs. 6 and 7. The first requirement is that mending must start and finish at a knot joining three strands or from a tag end leading from such a knot. This is necessary because only one end of mending twine is attached at a knot, and unless the knot is already composed of three unbroken strands of the original net, the repair will not have the required four strands radiating from each knot. The second requirement is that knots around the edges of the tear must have two—and only two—unbroken strands of the original net.

Fig. 17A—Shows a rectangular hole cut at a 45-degree angle to the mesh.

Fig. 17B—The patch is placed in position as shown here, in preparation for attachment.

Fig. 17C—The patch is now joined to the net by weaving from Figs. 1 to 24, where it is tied with a square knot. In the

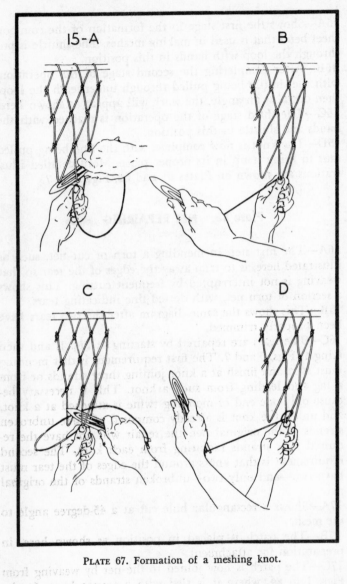

PLATE 67. Formation of a meshing knot.

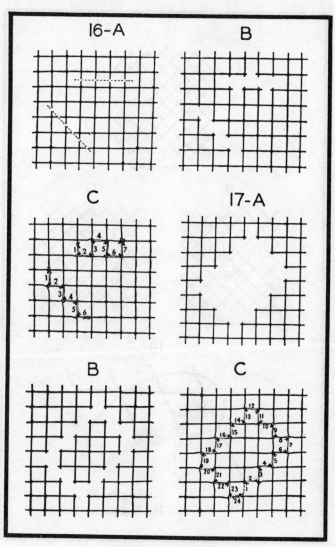

PLATE 68. Net repairing.

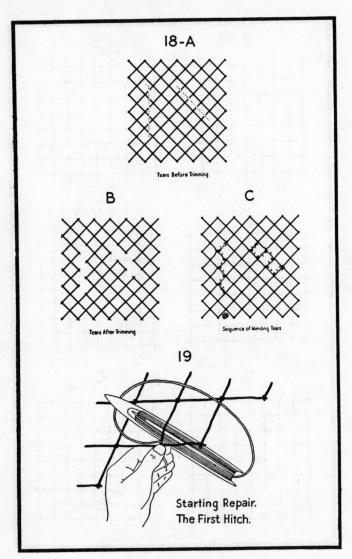

18-A

Tears Before Trimming

B

Tears After Trimming

C

Sequence of Mending Tears

19

Starting Repair.
The First Hitch.

PLATE 69. Net repairing continued.

process of altering diagonally woven nets where the rope edging is too short and requires lengthening to permit the nets to stretch taut when placed on flat tops, it is advisable to unsplice and remove rope edging, cutting points of attachment. Pull each edge of the ends of the net taut until mesh along it is closed. Then measure the edge. This will require one man at each end of an edge of the net. The same procedure is repeated on each of the net's edges. The length of the rope needed for each edge is three-quarters the length of the edge. Re-thread peripheral rope through edge meshes of net and resplice ends to finish the alteration.

Plate 69.   NET REPAIRING CONTINUED

Fig. 18A—Shows a vertical and diagonal tear before they are trimmed.

Fig. 18B—The same tear as it appears after being properly trimmed.

Fig. 18C—The proper sequence of mending the tears is illustrated here.

Fig. 19—Shows the first stage of the operation in starting repairs to weave the tear. If the mending starts at a knot where three strands join, the end of the twine should be tied on, as shown in this diagram and the two following diagrams.

Plate 70.   NET REPAIRING CONTINUED

Fig. 20—This shows a continuation of net repairing at the second stage of the operation. Note that the end of the twine is placed between two of the strands, the first hitch is made around these two strands and the second hitch is made around the middle strand only. The second hitch is made this way to bind the end of the twine more securely without excessively distorting the shape of the mesh. If the mending starts at a tag end, the end of the twine is tied to the tag end with a square knot.

Similar ties are used in finishing the repair. The sequence of weaving depends upon the shape and position of the tear with respect to the weave of the net, and must be sepa-

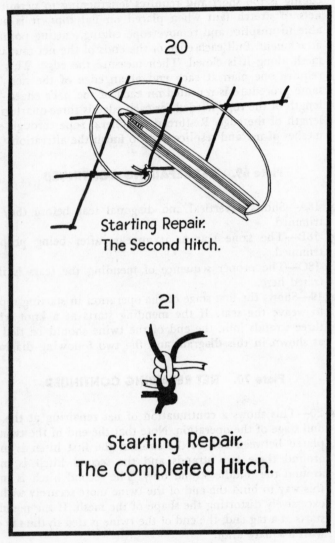

20

Starting Repair.
The Second Hitch.

21

Starting Repair.
The Completed Hitch.

PLATE 70. Net repairing continued.

rately determined for each job. The most convenient method for finding the proper sequence, and weaving the tear, is to spread the net out flat so that the meshes are square and then thread the twine through the meshes, without tying it at the knots, until the proper sequence is found by trial. The twine may then be cut and left in the net to guide the weaving. The guiding twine is removed after the repair is finished. With practice, one will become sufficiently expert to dispense with the use of the guiding twines. In adjusting a loop, care must be taken to note whether the loop forms one or two sides of a mesh and to adjust the size accordingly. Use either the right- or left-hand method of tying the knots, depending upon whether the twine goes from left to right or from right to left when the repair meshes are nearest the weaver. On some complicated tears, it will not be possible to trim the tear so that it may be rewoven in a continuous sequence without cutting out an excessive amount of net. In such cases, it is better to trim less extensively and weave several sequences, beginning and ending at three-strand knots, as already described.

Fig. 21—The finished knot in the preparation of repair work.

Plate 71. PATCHING A NET

Fig. 22A—When a net contains a large hole, it is quickest and easiest to insert a patch cut from a scrap net or to weave a patch separately and then insert it in the hole. The first step is to lay the net out and pull the meshes square. Then cut the hole out in a rough rectangular shape—45 degrees to the mesh—surrounded by knots joining two strands, as shown here. Note that a "three-strand knot" is not used for starting or finishing the insertion of the patch. This is because the weaving starts and finishes at the same knot when inserting a patch, rather than at different knots, as in mending a tear.

Fig. 22B—A rectangular patch is now cut or woven with one less "two-strand knot" on each side than on the corresponding side of the hole.

Fig. 22C—The patch is inserted in the net by weaving continuously around, as shown here, to complete the repair.

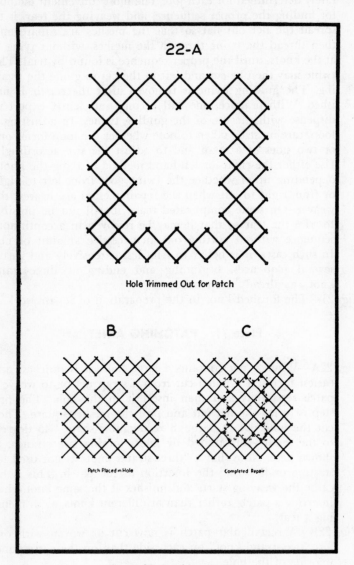

22-A

Hole Trimmed Out for Patch

B

Patch Placed in Hole

C

Completed Repair

PLATE 71. Patching a net.

Plate 72. MAKING A NARROWER OR WIDER ROW
OF MESHES, ETC.

Fig. 23—In order to reduce the amount of meshes or make a narrower row, pick up meshes *a* and *b* with the shuttle, instead of only *a*, as in the regular method. After these meshes have been picked up, the knot is tied, as shown at *c*, in the following illustration.

Fig. 24—To increase the amount of meshes or make the row wider, pick up mesh *d*, instead of going to mesh *b*, as in the usual method. The knot is tied at c and then meshing is resumed by proceeding to b for the next knot. Additional instructions of a similar nature are given on Plate 73, Fig. 35.

Fig. 25—Shows a 2-inch MESHING GAUGE or STICK with rounded corners. A type that is commonly used for network.

Fig. 26—The REEF KNOT is used for certain types of small meshwork where it is more suitable to use this kind of a knot instead of the sheet bend.

Fig. 27—The SHEET BEND is adapted to almost all kinds of network and is in common use everywhere for this purpose.

Fig. 28—Shows a 1-inch meshing gauge or stick with rounded corners.

Fig. 29—Shows 1½-inch meshing gauge or stick with square corners.

Fig. 30—A narrow needle or shuttle, ⅜ of an inch wide, 8 inches long.

Fig. 31—A small needle or shuttle, ⅞ of an inch wide, 6¾ inches long.

Fig. 32—A medium needle or shuttle, 1 inch wide, 8 inches long.

Fig. 33—A large needle or shuttle, 1⅛ inches wide, 9 inches long.

Plate 73. REDUCING AND INCREASING MESHES

Fig. 34—When it is necessary to decrease the size of the net by reducing two meshes into one, this operation is performed by tying two loops of meshes together, instead of one, as in the usual manner. The extent of the number of meshes tied double, in this fashion, depends upon how narrow the width of the net is going to be reduced. In order to keep the work

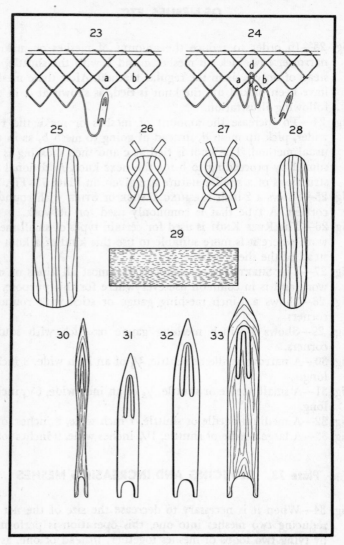

PLATE 72. Making a narrower or wider row of meshes, etc.

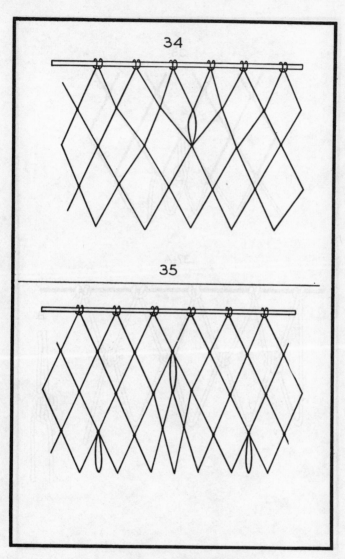

PLATE 73. Reducing and increasing meshes.

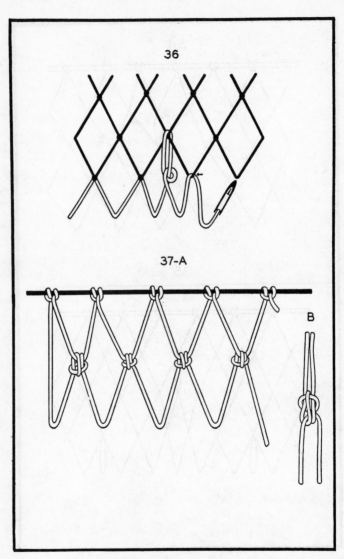

PLATE 74. Increasing meshes and lock knots.

uniform, it is best to place each reduced mesh an equal distance apart by spreading them across the net at certain intervals. This prevents the narrow spaces from bunching up and gives a more even effect to the work. See upper center part of illustration.

Fig. 35—To widen or increase the number of meshes in a row, additional loops are added by tying them in at different intervals, as illustrated, on each side at the bottom part of the net. These extra loops are picked up in the usual manner as the work progresses, thus adding additional meshes to each row in which they are used. See Plate 72, Fig. 24.

Plate 74. INCREASING MESHES AND LOCK KNOTS

Fig. 36—When REEF KNOTS are employed for making small meshes in certain types of shrimp nets, an open hitch such as that shown here will be found suitable for adding extra meshes in the net. The meshing is continued with another reef knot at the spot indicated by arrow. Meshes are reduced when using this method in the same manner as in Plate 72, Fig. 23. An additional illustration of a similar nature will also be found on Plate 73, Fig. 35.

Fig. 37A—Another FISH NET DESIGN formed with lock-knot sheet bends. The design is simple and may be followed easily. The knots are reversed from row to row or, in other words, they are tied in the opposite way in each successive row.

Fig. 37B—This shows the opposite or reverse method of constructing this knot opened up. It is a very effective method of making fish nets, as the knots hold fast and will not slip.

Plate 75. FISH AND LANDING NETS

Fig. 38—To start a FISH NET, such as that shown here, string up a length of cord and secure the end of the netting twine to the cord by means of a clove hitch. Any kind of netting needle or shuttle can be used that will perform the job properly. Commercial needles are usually $6\frac{1}{2}$ to 8 inches long; $\frac{5}{8}$ to $\frac{7}{8}$ of an inch wide, and approximately $\frac{1}{8}$ of an inch thick. The needle is filled by clove-hitching the end of the

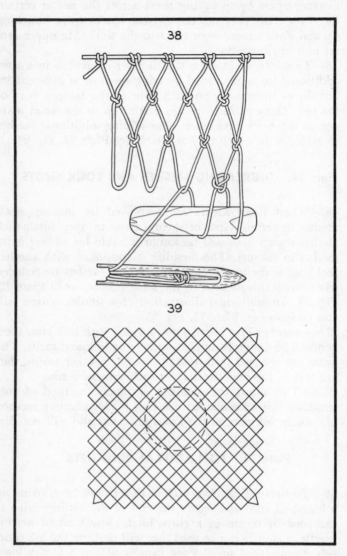

38

39

PLATE 75. Fish and landing nets.

twine around the central spine and leading it up the other side. Then bend the spine until its point projects just enough to permit the twine to be looped over the spine. The twine is then led back through the groove at the base of the needle to the starting side, where the process is repeated. The needle should be filled until the twine is approximately $1/4$ of an inch from the end of the spine. Leave about 24 inches of twine, not wound, on the needle. Then continue by using a meshing gauge, or stick, to measure the exact length and size of each successive mesh, after tying a clove hitch to the foundation cord each time a new mesh is formed. This process is repeated, working from left to right, until the required width of the net is reached. Starting back from right to left, begin forming sheet bends in the bottom of each mesh with a meshing shuttle, which is employed in connection with a meshing gauge of the proper size in order to insure meshes of uniform proportion, as shown in the illustration. As the work progresses, each knot is pulled taut and rows of meshes are worked back and forth until the net has reached the required size. If desired, the whole net can be turned over after each new row of meshes has been formed. The operation is thereby simplified in order to keep netting in one direction; either from left to right or vice versa. Note how the meshing shuttle is brought around the meshing gauge, and then up underneath and out through each succeeding mesh, after the sheet bend has been formed. It is then carried around and underneath the mesh with one hand, while holding the bottom of the mesh with the thumb and forefinger of the other hand. The meshing twine is then flipped over the shuttle as it is pulled through in order to form a new knot. Twelve to eighteen-thread medium-laid seine twine is the most commonly used line for making fish nets of this type.

Fig. 39—This illustrates the pattern or layout for a LANDING NET that is worked somewhat differently from Plate 76, Figs. 40A to G, although of the same general principle. The net is begun by making a series of 12 loops in a row, which is attached to a suspended cord by means of clove-hitching them to the cord in the usual manner. The operation is then continued until a series of 12 meshes, both vertical and hori-

171

zontal, have been formed. As the work proceeds, in order to avoid bulging corners in the net, work both the first and last mesh in top and bottom rows somewhat smaller than the average size. This can be accomplished by using a smaller meshing gauge when forming knots for such meshes. After the procedure already described has been completed, pick the net up in the middle, which is indicated by a circle on the interior of the illustration. It is then strung up by using a piece of line through the center.

Any one of the meshes may now be chosen to continue the work, as it is being carried around from left to right in a spiral manner. After one round has been worked, it is apparent that an uneven mesh will have a tendency to form. This is caused by the subsequent change from one method to another, which automatically takes place when working from the first circular row of meshes to the spiral rows that follow. As the work proceeds, this condition is gradually rectified and the net becomes more uniform in appearance, thereby giving it the effect of a natural pattern.

The same net can also be worked in circular fashion all the way down, instead of changing from circular to spiral style, as already described. This is accomplished by cutting the twine off after each round and starting over again on the last mesh that was formed. By following this style, the work will continue in a circle instead of spiral fashion, thus creating a more even appearance in the pattern.

Continue the work until the net reaches the proper dimensions, which is usually about 12 meshes wide and 12 meshes deep. In such nets as this, the mouth is generally made wider than the rest of the net. In order to do this, a larger meshing gauge or stick is used to form the necessary meshes in the usual manner. A meshing gauge of somewhat smaller proportion than the average will be necessary to form the meshes for the bottom part of the net in order to reduce the meshes down to the required size, which is ordinarily about ¾ of an inch square. The last meshes that are to be attached to the ring are made double. This is necessary to give the net added strength to withstand the wear at this point. When reducing or increasing the size of meshes, it is advisable to use a different size meshing gauge for each row until the meshes have been either reduced or increased to the required size. This gives a more even taper to the work.

Plate 76. INSTRUCTIONS ON HOW TO MAKE A LANDING NET

Figs. 40A to G—LANDING NETS may be constructed to suit individual requirements. Some fishermen prefer shallow nets with short handles, while others are in favor of much deeper nets with longer handles. This is largely a matter of choosing the kind of net the individual is accustomed to using or one which suits his needs best. Ordinary commercial nets purchased in stores are very shallow in depth, as a rule. However, they vary in type, size and shape of construction to such an extent that no uniform standard size or shape seems to have been definitely established to govern general practice in this field. No doubt the reason for this is that the requirements for such a wide variety of styles to satisfy the conveniences of every kind of fishing have made it necessary to provide the most useful and adaptable nets with which to serve every particular purpose and occasion. For instance, some nets have short wooden handles with egg-shaped metal rings, while others have long metal handles with round metal rings or wire frames to which the net is attached. On the other hand, still others have laminated wooden handles and wooden frames of various shapes and sizes, depending upon the type of net involved and for what general or particular purpose it is intended.

Numbered among the wide variety of different type nets in this field are such examples as the collapsible net, which has a triangular frame that folds flat against the handle. The frame and handle of this net are usually made of duralumin, and it is very light and handy to use. There is also a folding net that is made of light aluminum tubing with a sliding handle that locks with a thumbscrew. This kind of net usually has a wood handle. A flylyte net is another popular type. It has a bent wood frame joined with waterproof thong and tapered wooden handle. A featherweight boat net is also another addition to those previously described. This net has a triangular frame of hollow aluminum tubing with a

173

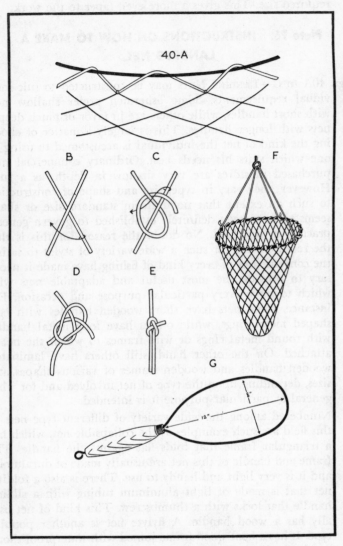

40-A

B C F

D E

G

3"

12"

PLATE 76. Instructions on how to make a landing net.

wooden handle, and is especially adapted to canoe and small boat fishing. The standard net, which is the last of several types described, is illustrated on the following plate.

There are likewise many different methods of making nets, just as there are different types of nets in use. The method described here will be found comparatively simple for either the beginner or experienced angler to follow in constructing his own landing net. Materials for a net of this type will require a piece of galvanized iron wire of about $1/8$ of an inch in diameter; a $5/8$-inch diameter brass ferrule $3/8$ of an inch long; one piece of soft wood $11/4$ x $11/4$ x $61/2$ inches, and one screw eye $1/4$ of an inch inside for the end of the handle, to which is attached a quick release snap that is fastened to the ring of the creel harness in order to carry the net. The net frame or ring should be almost egg-shaped and 8 inches wide by 12 inches long, with a ground bevel $1/2$ of an inch long on the point of each end. These should be bent or shaped parallel to each other for a distance of 2 inches beyond where each side of the frame comes together to form the projecting points that are inserted through the ferrule collar at the neck of the handle. After the net is attached to the frame, the points are then pushed in the handle until the frame fits up snug and close against the ferrule. Make the wooden handle about $61/2$ inches long and shape it with a slight taper at each end for a convenient grip. A coat of paint is next applied to the handle to finish the job. See Fig. 40G.

To begin the operation of forming the net, double a 12-foot piece of 12-thread seine twine by bringing it back in the form of a bight. This will make a 6-foot double strand. Next, take a single piece of twine about 4 feet long and form a sheet bend or common weaver's knot in the end of the bight of the double-strand part. See Figs. 40A to E. Leave about 3 or 4 inches of twine on the short end of the single part, after both parts are temporarily united in this fashion. A knot is used at this point in order to keep both parts of the line together while additional knots are being formed along the double-strand holding cord that will be attached to the frame of the net later on.

Now lay the joined parts out, with the long end of the doubled twine to the right and the long end of the single twine to the left. Bring the end of the single twine around to the right in order to start forming knots with the doubled part at 2-inch intervals. At this stage of the procedure, a sheet bend which is formed slightly different from Figs. 40B to E will be necessary to keep the work of a uniform character. Make a small eye by bringing the double part back and crossing it over itself, then run the end of the single part down through the eye of the double part, and encircle the top part which was used to form the cross with which the eye was made previously. After bringing the single twine around the double part, in the manner described, the end is then passed out through the eye from underneath, parallel to the way in which it was first run through. This will complete the knot. Draw each knot up snug by pulling on all four ends of the line as the work proceeds.

Continue to form knots at 2-inch intervals in this manner, until 3 or 4 inches from the end of the doubled twine. After the last knot has been tied, there will be a double row of meshwork on one side and a single row on the other. The work is now brought together and closed at the ends by first untying the starting knot which was made to attach both parts at the beginning. A sheet bend is then tied with the double line in the end of its own bight on the opposite part, where it had previously been joined with the single line which was untied for the purpose of the operation just described. The end of the single line that was originally attached to the bight of the double line, and later cast adrift, is now run down through the eye of the sheet bend that was formed with the double line on the opposite end of its own part. It is next doubled back around the free end of the double line, and then passed back through the eye parallel with the bight; or, in other words, to further simplify the explanation, the end of the single line is merely run through the knot by following the end of the bight, around which is part of the double line. The knot can now be pulled up snug and, after the net is attached to the tying ring, it is adjusted with proper care. The surplus ends are cut off after the net is completed.

From this point, the work is continued with the use of a

metal tying ring of about 10 inches in diameter, with a sliding ring to cover the ends where it is joined together. After the net has been placed on the tying ring and properly spaced around the ring, the work is then suspended with cords attached to a hook and anchored at a convenient working height from the ceiling. See Fig. 40F.

Meshing is now resumed with a single cord, allowing about $1\frac{1}{4}$ inches between each knot as the work progresses. After the net has been worked down to a depth of 12 or 14 inches, which is usually sufficient for a wading net, the meshes are shortened to about $\frac{1}{4}$ of an inch. The work is tapered down by skipping a mesh at equally spaced intervals on each side. When skipping meshes, be careful that opposite sides are worked in a corresponding manner, by tying 4 or 5 meshes after each mesh that has been skipped and then repeating the same procedure on the opposite side, and so on. This is necessary to keep the work of uniform appearance as the rows of meshes are being tapered down. A mesh is skipped by shortening the cord to about $\frac{1}{2}$ of an inch long between two ties. This space is not tied in when coming around with the next row of meshes.

After the net has been worked down and tapered into a conical shaped point at the bottom, it can be closed up when bringing the last meshes together by going direct from one mesh to the other, without allowing any slack for additional meshes, when tying the remaining knots. The end of the tying line can then be run from the last knot that is tied to the nearest opposite knot, and run back through this knot to form a double tie. This will close the end of the net in a neat, uniform manner. The double cord is now untied and the net is transferred from the tying ring to the net frame. The points of the frame are then inserted in the handle and the double cord is tied again in the usual manner to complete the job.

A complete net may be formed in this manner without the use of meshing shuttles or gauges. However, it is more practical to use such tools when doing most types of netting.

The following explanation includes instructions for making a landing net in a different manner from the preceding style. It is a popular method that is used by numerous fishermen who prefer a more professional type of net, which can be worked down to any depth desired by employing the same standard principles of construction that are used in commercial practice.

Make a chain of meshes to start the operation. The number of meshes required will depend upon the diameter desired for the mouth of the net. See Plates 61 to 63, Figs. 5 to 8. Medium-sized meshing shuttles and gauges are usually employed to start the mesh work, unless an exceptionally large mesh is desired, which will require larger working tools in proportion to the size of the mesh. After the starting chain has been completed, it is opened up and the top row of meshes are strung on a rod, as illustrated on Plate 64, Fig. 9. Work each row from left to right, which will simplify the operation. This can be accomplished by turning the work over after completing each new row, thus forming meshes by working in the same direction as the job progresses.

After the required amount of meshes has been completed, each succeeding row is reduced one mesh in order to start tapering the body of the net down to a cone-shaped point. The proper row to start reducing the mesh will have to be determined by making due allowance for the required depth and the diameter of the opening at the mouth. For nets of medium depth with a 12- to 14-inch opening at the mouth, which won't require as much length in meshwork to start with as a deeper net with a 15- or 16-inch opening, the fifth or sixth row will be approximately the right place to start reducing mesh. Whereas in a case where the latter size is required for the opening at the mouth and a much deeper net is preferred, meshes may start being reduced anywhere from the seventh to the ninth row, depending upon the desired depth. In this case the net, when completed, will hang about 30 to 33 inches deep, which will be sufficient for those who prefer the deeper type of net. See Plate 72, Fig. 23, for instructions on how to reduce meshes.

When reducing meshes, be careful to space them at certain intervals about the net, which will not bring the reduced meshes too close together. This will create an uneven appearance, whereas if they are spaced at uniform intervals, the net will look better and hang more evenly.

178

Meshing is continued until the taper of the net has been carried down far enough to satisfy the user's judgment. If in doubt about the proper place to stop work, the net may be removed from the rod at certain intervals and the sides of the net brought together in a tubular or sleevelike form, making due allowance at the same time for the additional meshwork that is necessary to close the sides of the net together, which will be explained later. If plenty of fullness is desired at the bottom, the tapering process should not be continued too far down, whereas if a more cone-shaped point is preferred, tapering will have to be governed accordingly. When the net has been tapered down far enough, take it off the holding rod. The two sides of the net are now brought together, with the edges within half a mesh width of each other to allow enough space for the added meshwork with which it is closed. To start the closing operation hang the net on a nail in a horizontal position at a convenient working height. This will support the work as the finishing mesh is being woven into the sides to close the body into a tubular or cylindrical shape with an open bottom.

After the net is hung properly and the sides have been brought together, as previously described, the work is continued by weaving an extra mesh through the complete length of the sides. This is done in the following manner: Start at the top end at the point of the outside mesh on the right side of the first row on the lower side of the work. Pull each mesh out to form a square before tying the knot each time. The proper point or corner at which to tie the knot can be determined more easily in this manner. Now proceed directly across to the opposite or upper side and tie the knot at the outside point in the same manner, taking care at the same time to allow plenty of fullness in the mesh to correspond with the other outside meshes.

Continue by working toward the left or bottom end, going diagonally across from the corner of one mesh to the corner of the next mesh, after they have been pulled out in the shape of a square. In this manner, the extra meshes or squares that are created by the interwoven sides can be worked into the same size pattern as the others by allowing for the proper space between ties. As the work progresses,

179

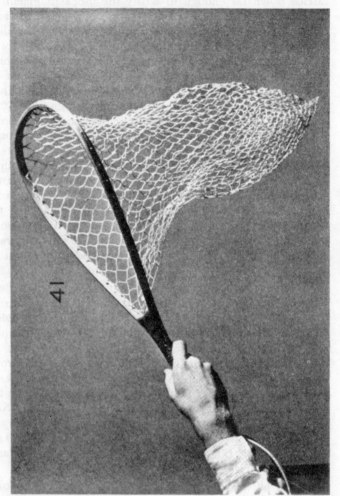

PLATE 77. A standard landing net.

it will be necessary to shift the body of the net on the nail to keep it hanging properly. After the sides have been woven together with an equal amount of fullness on the outside opposite end of the work, as at the starting point, the next step will be the closing operation at the bottom of the net. This is accomplished in a simple way by using a split brass ring of about one inch in diameter or slightly less to which are attached the corners of all the remaining bottom meshes. If no split brass ring is available, a solid ring may be used by employing an extra piece of cord which is tied to the ring and run through each mesh and back through the ring two or three times, then pulled up taut and securely hitched. Follow the same procedure until all the meshes have been lashed to the ring in this manner.

Medium-laid 12-thread seine twine is the most practical line to use for nets of this type. See Plate 56, Figs. 7 to 10 for the proper rules for mesh measurements and hanging nets.

Figs. 40B to E—The formation of a weaver's knot, which is a common sheet bend, the most useful tie for net making.

Fig. 40B—This shows the strands crossed to begin the knot, with the arrow indicating the next step.

Fig. 40C—After the end has been brought around, the other end is brought down and through bight—shown by drawn line.

Fig. 40D—After this tuck has been made, draw out the slack.

Fig. 40E—The completed knot turned over and pulled taut.

Plate 77.   A STANDARD LANDING NET

Fig. 41—A LAMINATED WOOD FRAME NET such as this is a standard commercial market type that is ideal for stream fishing. A scored groove 1/12 of an inch wide and 1/16 of an inch deep encircles the outer edge of the frame; ⅛-inch holes are bored at 1-inch intervals along this groove around the entire length of the frame. A small line is then used for a jackstay by running it inside the groove and picking up the meshes which are stuck through the holes to connect with the jackstay as it is passed around the length of the frame. It is then tied off in the center near the fore part of the handle. The bag is made of cotton thread mesh in the usual manner. The handle has a wound grip and an elastic cord attached.

PRESERVATION AND CARE OF FISH NETS

By Frank E. Firth and Carl B. Carlson, Technologists
Division of Commercial Fisheries

WARTIME dislocations have seriously decreased the supply of webbing available for fish nets. If fishermen are to continue maximum efficiency of operation, it is now imperative that they use every means available to extend the life of their nets.

Aside from normal losses, all fishing gear must eventually be replaced because of chafing, oxidation, and bacterial action. Continuing investigations by the Fish and Wildlife Service indicate that by properly treating nets, these causes of deterioration can be materially reduced. The suggestions in this article are intended to reacquaint fishermen with some of the easier and more practical methods of preservation which are not unduly time-consuming.

The three general types of preservatives in common use are coal tar, copper-containing compounds, and tanbark extracts, which may be used singly or in combination. Coal tar, and to some extent pine tar, are used primarily on "heavy nets"—pounds, traps, otter trawls, and seines—where abrasion is an important factor. "Light nets"—gill and trammel nets, and light seines—are of soft texture, and require a nonhardening preservative.

TAR TREATMENT

Application of coal tar offers a simple and effective means of preserving heavy nets. Fisheries specifications coal tar,[1] a vertical retort tar, sometimes called seine tar, is recommended

---

[1]Fisheries Specification tar A (American Society for Testing Materials Specification R. T.), as recommended for use on fish nets by the United States Fish and Wildlife Service:

Water, not over 2 per cent by volume.
Specific gravity, minimum 1.10 at 25° C.
Specific viscosity at 40° C. 18 to 25.
Total bitumen, minimum 88 per cent.
Softening point or residue 35° C. to 65° C.

Total distillation by weight to:
170° C. 5 per cent maximum.
270° C. 30 per cent maximum.
300° C. 40 per cent maximum.

for best results. This product may be obtained through most supply stores. If for any reason it is necessary or desirable to thin the tar, water-gas-tar oil with a viscosity of less than 2.00 at 40° C. (Engler) is recommended.

The tar should be heated in a water jacket or steam-coil heated tank. If the tarring must be done in direct-fired receptacles, such as iron kettles or cut-off oil barrels, the tar should be continuously stirred to prevent local overheating and charring of the webbing. The temperature of the tar should be between 150° F. and 180° F. This temperature range is adequate to give good penetration and will not burn or char the webbing. Common practice has been to test temperature by touch, but this is very unreliable.

Nets should be clean and thoroughly dry before the tar treatment is applied. The steam pipes should be checked for leaks, since any escaping steam will form a film of water on the surface of the tar, which will wet the net and cause inadequate penetration wherever this water absorption occurs.

Three-minute immersion should insure adequate penetration. Many fishermen consider it good practice to run the freshly tarred netting through a wringer to remove the excess tar, then immerse the tarred net in fresh water for at least 12 hours to leach out water-soluble products considered harmful to netting. The netting should be hung in a shaded place with free air circulation, because direct sunlight in the drying process is harmful.

Various modifications of the coal-tar treatment for netting have been developed, and several good commercial products are available through fishery supply houses. Experiments by the Fish and Wildlife Service indicate that a mixture of copper oleate or naphthenate, benzene, and coal tar, which can be readily prepared by fishermen, is an excellent treatment to reduce fouling The proportions are 4½ gallons of benzene and 5½ gallons of coal tar for each 15 pounds of copper oleate or naphthenate. The copper compound should contain at least 6 to 8 per cent copper, and be dissolved in the benzene before being added to the coal tar. A mixture of this type has the advantage of giving satisfactory penetration without heating and, because of its highly inflammable properties, should be kept away from flame.

Treatment with this mixture results in a lighter and more flexible net, and greatly reduced drying time. The preservative action will be improved if the nets are stored in the shade or under shelter, because sunlight causes the copper oleate or naphthenate to lose its effectiveness. Periodic application of the mixture is recommended.

Excellent results have been obtained in experiments with chrome-tanned netting subjected to a final tarring treatment.

COPPER TREATMENT

Copper treatments are generally indicated when a light, soft, pliable twine is desirable. Copper oleate and copper naphthenate are widely used for preserving light nets, but neither is a permanent preservative. Because it is slightly soluble in water, the compound gradually leaches out of the net; thus the treatment must be reapplied periodically.

The copper oleate or naphthenate should have a copper content of at least 6 or 8 per cent and from 1 to 5 pounds of the paste may be used per gallon of kerosene, depending upon the use of the gear. Superior penetration is obtained when the gear is immersed for several hours rather than the customary 5 to 15 minutes. Experiments indicate that the life of netting may be nearly doubled by a "refreshing" treatment, consisting of 1 or 2 pounds of copper compound per gallon of solvent applied every 30 days for salt-water use and more often for fresh water.

Nets treated with copper compounds should be stored in a well-ventilated, shady place, as direct sunlight oxidizes the preservative and renders it crumbly and useless. In addition, the twine itself is weakened as a result of this oxidation.

Copper sulphate (bluestone) exercises a marked preserving action on linen thread and gives fair results with cotton. Nets and lines periodically treated with bluestone take on a blue color, indicating that there is some fixing of the copper compound. Since it has remarkable slime and dirt removing properties, however, bluestone should be regarded as a cleansing agent rather than as a preservative.

A dip of common, copper bottom-paint has given excellent results on pound nets where barnacle and vegetable growths have proved irksome. As dried copper paint is quite brittle, any surface accumulation will disappear if the twine is subjected to much bending. Copper paint has been quite successfully used as a preservative for lacing twine on seines, thus avoiding the undesirable characteristics of freshly tarred twine.

Oxidation of textile fibers is accelerated in the presence of copper compounds, and deterioration results. Copper treatment, other than with bluestone, therefore, is not recommended within 15 days prior to the end of the season.

TANNING TREATMENTS

Treatment of netting with cutch or tanbark extracts is one of the oldest methods of preservation in use, and is still highly recommended where a light net is desired and color is not objectionable. Tanning is quite simple if the necessary tanks are available.

The treating solution is made by dissolving cutch extract in boiling water in the proportion of 6 pounds to 12 gallons. If cutch is not available, or tanbark is preferred, 13 pounds of oak or hemlock bark may be substituted in the same volume of water. It is recommended that the net be immersed in the near-boiling solution for 12 hours. A direct-fired kettle may be used for this purpose, but a water-jacketed tank or one heated with steam coils is preferable. When direct-fired kettles are used, a grid is recommended to prevent the net from coming into contact with the bottom of the kettle. If no further treatment is contemplated, the netting should be thoroughly dried in a shady place until ready for use. The tanning solution may be stored for subsequent treatment, but some cutch and water should be added to bring it to original strength and volume before re-use.

The gear should be treated at regular intervals to give maximum life. The frequency of treatment depends upon the conditions of use and the amount of foreign material. A few fishermen give their nets a refreshing treatment after 6 days' use, but the average is probably nearer 25 days. It is recommended that successive treatments be applied before there is noticeable fading of color. If the net is exposed to severe slime conditions, common salt should be sprinkled throughout the net at the end of each day's operations and the net be retanned at least every two weeks.

To effect a superior tanning, the freshly tanned and drained net may be given a subsequent chrome fixing bath. This will increase the stability of the tanning, resulting in better preservation. The bath is made up by dissolving 4 ounces of potassium dichromate (redstone) in 12 gallons of boiling water. The net should be boiled for 15 minutes, then immediately given a rinse in clear water. This solution need not be saved, as a fresh solution must be prepared for each refreshing treatment.

CLEANING OF NETS

There is no known preservative which will protect nets against damage from lack of cleanliness or careless storage. All gear freshly fished is more or less contaminated with fish slime and other matter which should be removed or neutralized as quickly as practical. The cleaning agents in most common use are brine, bluestone, and lime.

The immediate washing and drying of nets is often impractical in some fisheries and impossible in others, but a simple brine treatment is quite valuable. The nets may be dipped in strong brine or sprinkled with generous quantities of coarse common salt, and sea water or brine poured over them. This method is generally used to preserve the purse-seine nets of the menhaden and mackerel fisheries.

Treatment of nets with bluestone solution is universally

used and highly recommended by Pacific coast fishermen for prolonging the life of all types of fishing gear. As stated previously, this treatment has a pronounced cleaning action in addition to being a preservative. The strength of the solution depends upon the preference of the individual fisherman and his judgment as to the amount of slime and sediment on the gear. Generally, 25 to 40 pounds of bluestone (copper sulphate) is dissolved in about 200 gallons of water. Exact proportions are seldom used, the strength being determined by the color of the solution. The most common procedure is to place the bluestone in a burlap sack and work it through water in a suitable small boat or tank. Fifty or a hundred pounds of salt may also be added, but this is not considered necessary by most fishermen. The solution may be poured over the net or the net immersed in it, but there is evidence that better cleansing and preservation result by submerging the net. Large nets, such as seines, are dipped a portion at a time by letting them into and pulling them out of the boat (skiff). or tank. It is recommended that the net be washed or used within 36 hours after such dipping. The bluestone treatment should be applied at least every two weeks and, if slime conditions are severe, the nets should be "salted" at the conclusion of each day's operation. Nets which receive these additional bluestone and salt treatments will last 3 to 4 seasons in the salmon, and 2 to 3 seasons in the herring and pilchard fisheries.

Lime water is used extensively by gill-netters in the Great Lakes, and to some extent by New England gill-net fishermen to clean their nets. Lime water is easily prepared by keeping a few inches of slacked lime in a barrel or tank, adding as much water as possible, and stirring thoroughly. After the milk color disappears, the clear solution is ready for use. Immediately after removing the fish, lime water is poured over the nets, which are then rinsed with clear water. Two pails of lime water are adequate for a small gill net. Soaking nets for a day or two in clear, fresh water, just prior to storage, is a simple and very effective means of ridding them of any marine growths which may have become attached to the webbing.

STORAGE OF NETS

Improper storage of nets invariably results in considerable damage to gear and consequent loss to the owner. Nets washed immediately after use and dried in the shade keep their strength remarkably well. While exposure to sunlight for several hours acts as a strong deterrent to destructive bacteria, prolonged exposure is quite injurious. Tests also show that industrial gases containing sulphurous fumes may cause serious damage to wet linen, with cotton netting affected to a lesser extent. A wet net piled up under a tight cover may be quickly ruined by bacteria and mildew.

Nets should be stored loosely suspended in a well-ventilated shelter with free circulation of air. If it is necessary to heap the nets, liberal quantities of salt should be used between the layers of twine.

The necessity for longer life from fish nets cannot be overemphasized.

USE OF COPPER OLEATE AS A NET PRESERVATIVE

Reprinted Courtesy U. S. Bureau of Fisheries
Fish and Wild Life Service, Washington, D. C.

Additional experiments made by the Bureau of Fisheries and the results of recent interviews with fishermen who are employing copper oleate in the New England and Middle Atlantic States disclose certain items of possible interest to manufacturers and users of this product.

The survey showed that copper oleate is being used extensively by the lobster and pound-net fishermen from Maine to Long Island. They have, with few exceptions, had excellent results.

The principal suggestions from users of copper oleate were: (1) Something should be done to keep copper oleate from washing out of the webbing to the extent that it now does; (2) There is need of some substance which when combined with copper oleate will give it more body so that the webbing will be better protected from mechanical wear; and (3) When copper oleate is used on seines some substance should be added which will prevent the slipping of knots when the seine is hauled.

With respect to the first of these suggestions, one must remember that if copper oleate is to successfully prevent growth it is necessary for it to be at least slightly soluble in water. An entirely inert substance would not preserve at all. It is doubtful, therefore, if it would be advisable to decrease the solubility of copper oleate to any great extent. The bureau has conducted some experiments which have indicated that if the solubility is appreciably decreased copper oleate is less effective as an antifouling agent.

In regard to the second suggestion, it has been found from the bureau's experiments that a mixture of copper oleate and coal tar makes an excellent preservative, in fact, the most effective of any tested. This treatment would also eliminate the slipping of knots. Where considerable increase in weight and stiffness is objectionable such a treatment, of course, would not be permissible.

These objections from the users of copper oleate are important. However, if a serious effort is put forth to overcome them it might be possible to do so or at least to minimize them. The bureau will naturally undertake to develop means of overcoming these defects.

The fishermen were about equally divided in their opinions as to whether gasoline or kerosene gave better results as a solvent. The bureau is still of the belief, however, that gasoline is more satisfactory. It was also found that in most cases better results were obtained when the net or webbing was allowed to steep in the solution for several hours, preferably over night, instead of 5 or 10 minutes as was first recommended by the bureau.

It is well known that the practice of drying nets on the sand exposed to the hot sun is a very bad one. There seems to be no question but that the life of the webbing is greatly shortened by this procedure and such treatment seems particularly bad where copper oleate is used. Fishermen state that if webbing

189

which has been treated with copper oleate is allowed to remain thus exposed for two or three days the copper oleate becomes crumbly, of a very pale green color, and apparently loses its value as a preservative. Netting should be hung so as to have free circulation of air about it during drying.

Further experiments by the bureau have indicated that the life of twine exposed under most unfavorable water conditions may be more than doubled by removing the twine every 30 days, drying, and retreating it with the copper oleate. Particular attention is called to this result. From the first the bureau has advocated frequent treatment of webbing which is continuously submerged or otherwise subjected to long exposure in water. It is certainly cheaper to treat netting often than it is to buy new.

Experiments also have shown that there is a very marked difference in the effect which certain waters have on twine during like periods of different years. For example, twine submerged at a certain point in Lake Erie underwent a very marked diminution of strength during certain months of one year, but when exposed at the same place during the same season of the following year only slight deterioration resulted.

The experience of users of copper oleate in New Jersey waters has not been wholly satisfactory. The bureau is in no position to state definitely to what cause the unsatisfactory results obtained were due. Pound-net fishermen in this region stated that the copper oleate purchased by them washed out after 10 to 14 days in the water and that the nets fouled very badly after about two weeks. Some of the fishermen attribute the trouble to the fact that the water off the coast of New Jersey contains large quantities of oil and sewage which come down along the coast from New York Bay, and may act adversely on copper oleate. The quality of some of the copper oleate used has also been questioned. One fisherman stated that analyses made of three or four samples of copper oleate purchased from various concerns in some cases contained but 1 or 2 per cent of copper. Since copper is the active principle of copper oleate, it can be readily understood why copper oleate of the quality mentioned above, if used, would be much less efficient than that containing the proper percentage of copper (6 to 7 per cent).

In conclusion, it may be said that although copper oleate has certain limitations it has proven its worth for various types of gear and is being quite widely used. It is believed that as present objections are overcome, modifications of its use for different types of gear developed, and its real economy demonstrated, its use will be much more widespread. The bureau will welcome reports from users of copper oleate as to the results of their experience, especially improvements in its use or difficulties encountered. There are also some features of net preservation, other than the matter of prevention of deterioration which might be brought to attention. In judging the merits of copper oleate the fisherman is urged to consider the following points: Are nets treated with copper oleate more effective in taking fish? Is there less labor involved in handling such nets in the water?

NET PRESERVATIVE TREATMENTS

MORE LIFE FROM FISH NETS

*By W. T. Conn, Technologist, U. S. Bureau of Fisheries
Fish and Wild Life Service, Washington, D. C.*

It is known that for each dollar American fishermen receive for their catch, 20 cents is paid out for nets. All gear is going to wear out and some losses cannot be avoided, but it is believed that this article will assist many fishermen to reduce the cost of fishing by increasing the service life of nets.

PRESERVING HEAVY NETS

The term "heavy nets" is used to designate pound and trap nets, heavy seines and other gear ordinarily tarred by American fishermen.

Investigation by the Bureau of Fisheries indicates that the agency most destructive to nets kept in water for considerable periods is a microscopic form of life that digests (eats) cotton or similar material. But if the cotton is properly dyed or otherwise chemically changed in character, it is much less attractive as food

191

for the microorganism. When this chemically treated cotton thread is properly tarred, it has a much longer average service life than raw cotton thread of the same size tarred in the same way.

Except in a very few foul waters, the most practical chemical treatment for heavy net cotton is good barking or cutching. Cutched twine can be bought from manufacturers of nets or can be prepared as follows:

Dissolve cutch extract[1] in boiling water in the proportion of 6 pounds extract to 100 pounds (about 12 gallons) of water. Avoid burning of the extract by adding a portion of the boiling water to the extract in an unheated pail or tub, stirring until the extract is dissolved, then mixing the strong solution into the balance of the water, with thorough stirring.

The net is placed in the cutch solution, which is kept close to the boiling point for 12 hours. If necessary, keep the net under the solution by weights or other means. The net can then be lifted and allowed to drain back into the tank.

A fixing bath is then prepared as follows: Use a steam-heated wooden tank, or iron kettle heated by fire. In each 100 pounds (about 12 gallons) of boiling water, dissolve 4 ounces potassium bichromate (also known as "redstone"). Stir until the chemical is thoroughly dissolved and have the solution boiling.

The drained but wet tanned net is placed in the fixing bath, where it is boiled for 15 minutes. The net must immediately be thoroughly rinsed in clear water; it is then well dried.

The leftover tanning liquor can be kept for future use by either adding it to fresh solution or by restoring the original volume and strength by addition of water and cutch extract. In ordinary practice this is done by keeping a sample of the original liquor in a clear flat bottle. Add water and chemical to the cutch tank, stirring until a sample of the new liquor in a duplicate bottle is of the same color as the original.

The fixing bath solution must be made up fresh each time webbing is put into it. After webbing is boiled, the leftover solution is useless and should be drained off and thrown away.

The extra cost of cutching a heavy net that is to be

tarred afterward is less than 15 per cent. Tests made in various fishing waters indicate that for this small additional cost, an average increase in service life of over 100 per cent may be expected; that is, a net cutched before tarring should give double the life of a net tarred without cutching.

In muddy river waters, tarred-cutched twine, while superior to plain tarred, will not resist rotting as well as chrome-tarred twine. The chrome is applied by successive treatments as follows:

1. Prepare a solution in the following proportions: In each 100 pounds (about 12 gallons) of water, dissolve $\frac{1}{2}$ pound white soap and 3 pounds washing soda. Boil the net in this solution for 5 minutes, then immediately rinse well in cold water.

2. Prepare a solution in the following proportions: In each 100 pounds (about 12 gallons) of water, dissolve 2 pounds tannic acid. Soak the washed net in this solution for 8 hours at a temperature of about 160° F.

3. Prepare a solution in the following proportions: In each 100 pounds (about 12 gallons) of water, dissolve 1 pound tartar emetic[2] and heat to 160° F.; transfer the net from the tannic acid solution (without rinsing) to this one and continue the same heat for 1 hour.

4. Prepare a solution in the following proportions, using a lead lined tank or wooden tank heated by brass or lead covered steam pipes: In each 100 pounds (about 12 gallons) of water, dissolve 1 pound potassium bichromate (redstone) and 3 pounds copper sulphate (bluestone); heat to a simmering temperature and add 2 pounds (about 1 quart) 30° acetic acid. Stir well, and transfer the net from the tartar emetic bath (without rinsing) to this solution and soak for 20 minutes at a simmering heat. The net should then be immediately and thoroughly rinsed in clear water and well dried.[3] The net is then tarred.

TARRING

Good tarring of nets depends upon buying the right grade of tar and upon careful tarring of the nets. Direct-fired tar kettles (those where fire is applied directly under the kettle) may ruin good tar, and have cost fishermen fortunes in burned and scorched nets.

Tar will not penetrate cotton thread until it is heated above 180° F. Cotton begins to scorch at 220° F. and the tar should never be hotter than this. Temperature of the tar should be checked by a thermometer and, if possible, kept between 200° F. and 215° F. The net must be kept in the tar for at least 3 minutes to insure penetration.

The foregoing principles apply to all tarring. To get maximum service from heavy nets, use Fisheries Specification Tar[4] on well cutched or chromed webbing. This tar has been found satisfactory for general work. If any tar is considered too heavy, it should be thinned with water gas or tar oil.

Care should be used in the storage of tarred webbing. It should never be heaped up when freshly tarred. After use, if heaping is necessary, a generous quantity of coarse salt should be used to separate the threads. Direct sunshine rots nets. The best storage for tarred nets is to hang them up under shelter where they will be dried by the air but protected from the sun.

PRESERVING LIGHT NETS

The ordinary gill net may be taken as a type of this class of gear, but for the purpose of preservation, the term "light nets" may include all gear not tarred.

Nearly all gill nets are in the water for relatively short periods and extensive observation has shown that generally water damage is slight. All gear freshly fished is more or less contaminated with fish slime which should be removed as quickly as possible by rinsing the net with lime water, followed by a clear water rinse. Lime water is easily prepared by keeping a few inches of slacked lime in a barrel and adding as much fresh or salt water as possible, with stirring. After the milky color disappears, the clear solution is ready for use. Fishermen on Lake Erie carry a barrel with lime in the bottom and filled with water to about 8 inches from the top. As soon as the nets are cleared of fish, two pails of the lime water are poured over each box of nets, which are then rinsed with clear water. These nets are relatively free from the odor of fish and are giving excellent service.

Direct sunshine ruins dry gill nets. Tests of the Bureau of Fisheries indicate that the damage caused by drying 40/3 linen in the sun on the North Carolina coast between April 1 and September 30, 1933, amounted to over 5 cents per hour for each $100 of linen. Linen of the same stock wet by rain at the same time, but dried in the shade, was almost as good as new after the six-months test, 36/6 cotton exposed to the sun and rain at the same time rotted almost as badly, but cotton of the same stock exposed only to the rain, but dried in the shade, was stronger after six months than when new. Tests south of the Carolinas had increased sun damage while those north indicated serious but less damage from sun exposure. Detailed investigation of one New England gill-netter indicates that if the nets on this boat were dried in shade, the owner would save $2.00 each summer fishing day.

ALL NETS SHOULD BE DRIED AND STORED WHERE THE SUN WILL NOT SHINE ON THEM, UNLESS THE OWNER IS PREPARED TO LOSE MONEY NEEDLESSLY.

When color of light nets is of no consequence, well-cutched gear gives service somewhat superior to plain twine. When the color fades, it should be given a freshening treatment, as described under "heavy nets."

For light nets that are subjected to long periods of water exposure, the best preservative is chroming, as described under "Preserving heavy nets" in numerous submersion tests in all waters, chromed cotton has given over 7 times the life of untreated cotton and over 4 times the life of cutched cotton.

An inferior, but less complicated preservative treatment for light nets subjected to long periods of water exposure is prepared by dissolving a special copper naphthenate ("Conapthan") in kerosene in the proportion of 30 pounds of the naphthenate in 70 pounds (about 10½ gallons) kerosene. When fishing in cold water, a further improvement of service can be obtained by adding 5 ounces antioxidant (No. 10 oil soluble antioxidant made by the R. T. Vanderbilt Co., East Norwalk, Connecticut) to each 100 pounds of the preservative. After the chemicals are completely dissolved in the hot kerosene, the net should be immersed for 3 minutes at a temperature around 200° F., spread out and dried in shade. This treatment, like others of its type, may cause knot slipping in new nets and it is recommended for use only on webbing in which the knots are well set up.

REDUCING FOULING OF NETS

The control of growths on nets has been the subject of extensive investigation with only partial success. Some fouling is mechanical and at the present time cannot be prevented. Saltwater growths are subject to extreme variations, and can be eliminated generally only by sacrificing the strength of the webbing. Research by the Bureau of Fisheries has disclosed that salt-water weed growth on tarred webbing can be very materially reduced and shell growths somewhat lessened, with increase in service strength of the webbing, by thoroughly mixing into each 100 pounds (about 12 gallons) of tar, $3\frac{1}{2}$ pounds of a mercury compound[5] known as "Du Pont Marine Weed Killer," manufactured by E. I. du Pont de Nemours and Company, Inc., Wilmington, Delaware. THIS CHEMICAL IS EXTREMELY POISONOUS IF TAKEN INTO THE MOUTH AND MUST BE HANDLED WITH THE GREATEST CARE. Incomplete tests indicate that it does not affect fish gilled in webbing, but the Bureau of Fisheries will not be responsible for any result of its use.

[1]Thirteen pounds oak or hemlock bark or three pounds quercitron crystals may be used instead of six pounds cutch extract in each twelve gallons of water. If quercitron crystals are used, it is recommended that they be placed in a coarse bag and allowed to dissolve through the cloth.
[2]Tartar emetic is poisonous if taken internally. Care should be used in handling.
[3]Application for a nonroyalty public patent on this process is pending.
[4]Application for nonroyalty public patent has been made for applying tar to a cutched net.
[5]An application is pending for a nonroyalty public patent covering a mixture of tar and certain mercury compounds to form a preservative.

THE TANNING OR BARKING OF NETS

By W. T. Conn, Technologist, U. S. Bureau of Fisheries
Fish and Wild Life Service, Washington, D. C.

The barking or tanning of fish nets is perhaps the oldest principle for the preservation of fishing gear, dating back to prehistoric times and today practiced with various modifications among fishermen in all parts of the world.

Barking is used without further treatment upon light nets and seines in fisheries where the dark brown color of the webbing is not objectionable, and where the nets are not subjected to constant exposure in the water. In the case of seines subjected to rough handling, webbing that has no treatment other than tanning may suffer serious mechanical wear.

While many detailed methods of the general principle of tanning nets are in use, the following procedure illustrates accepted practice combined with the results of research by this Bureau.

Dissolve cutch extract[1] in boiling water in the proportion of 6 pounds to 100 pounds (about 12 gallons) of water. Burning of the extract can be avoided by adding a portion of the boiling water to the extract in an unheated vessel, then mixing the strong solution into the balance of the water, with thorough stirring. When the chemical is completely dissolved, the net is immersed (with weights, if necessary) and allowed to stand for at least 12 hours, with the bath kept at a temperature just below the boiling point. The net is then raised above the solution and allowed to drain back into the container.

For the purpose of securing the greatest benefit from the tanning, the net must be subjected to a fixing bath which may be prepared as follows: For each 100 pounds (about 12 gallons) of boiling water allow 4 ounces potassium bichromate (also known as "redstone"). The chemical should be completely dissolved and the solution well mixed before use.

The drained but wet tanned net is placed in the fixing bath, which is boiled for 15 minutes. The net must immediately be thoroughly rinsed in clear water; it is then ready for use.

The leftover tanning liquor can be kept for future use by either adding it to fresh solution or by restoring the original volume and strength by the addition of water and cutch extract. In ordinary practice this is done by keeping a sample of the original liquor in a clear flat bottle and adding water and chemical until the new liquor in a duplicate bottle is of the same color as the original.

The spent liquor from the fixing bath is useless and should be thrown away.

When the above treatment is used for light nets or seines which are not tarred, it is recommended that the preservative process be repeated when the webbing is materially faded. Some fishermen give their nets a freshening treatment after 6 days' use, but this is not common practice. Possibly a freshenening treatment after 25 days' use is average practice.

Research of this Bureau has demonstrated upon heavy commercial nets that when Fisheries Specification Tar is properly applied to a well tanned net, the latter gives superior service when subjected to water exposure for many months. The mechanical protection afforded by the tar resists abrasion of the webbing.

Ropes either of manila or cotton have increased life when subjected to the above process.

1See p. 196 (footnote 1).

198

Index

Anchors
  how to prevent fouling, 117
  slingstone, 79
Attachments
  dropper point, 79
  line to swivel, 77
  swivel, spinner or ringed hook, 25
Bait Grapple, 131
Belaying
  eye spliced line, 129
  making an eye fast to a belaying
    pin, 129
  —second method, 129
  rope on a belaying pin, 129
Bends
  anchor, 35
  —and bowline, 37
  —double, 35
  —opposite way, 35
  —rolling, 37
  barrel knot, 5, 62
  —variations, 67
  becket, 59
  blood knot, 5, 6, 23, 62
  —rolling, 67
  double carrick, 60
  Englishman's, 60
  fisherman's, 35, 60
  —double, 5
  gut, 62
  —leader, 60, 62
  halibut, 60
  mogul, 37
  Napoleon, 115
  overhand, 60
  reef knot, 23
  right-handed sheet, 59
  ring, 62
  sheet, 165
  —double, 7
  —on a bight, 60
  —slip, 60
  —single, 7
  single riverman's, 60
  —double, 60
  —with bow, 60
  stunsail halyard, 41
  true lover's, 60
  water knot, 62

Bowlines
  anchor, 119
  French, 57
  heaving line, 127
  ordinary, 5, 7, 79
  —on the bight, 59
  Spanish, 59
Braids
  four-strand, 25
Chairs
  rigging for a boatswain's, 123
Coachwhipping
  four-strand, 119
Coils
  coiling down rope, 103
  flemishing down rope, 101
  —second method, 103
  heaving line, 103
  making up a gasket, 103
  overlapping figure-of-eight, 105
  sash cord, 103
Connections
  attaching a dropper strand, 21
  figure-of-eight, 21
  safety pin and loose hook, 15
Coxcombs
  three-strand common, 119
Crowns
  three-strand, 81
Eyes
  artificial or spindle, 113
Fastenings
  single chain, 125
  temporary, 39
  wire to swivel, 15
Fenders
  fisherman's, 109
  spiral, 121
Gaff
  handmade, 73
Gaskets
  making up, 103
Grommets
  hemp laid long spliced, 94
  three-strand, 94
Hawsers
  faking down, 105
  placing over a bollard, 125
  securing on a bollard, 125
  three on one bollard, 125

199

Hitches
  Arizona handcuff, 53
  backhanded sailor's, 34
  —second method, 34
  bulkhead, 101
  —second method, 103
  buntline, 37
  buoy, 35
  clove, 33, 39
  —reverse, 33
  —slip, 42
  coil, 103
  cow, 33
  double becket, 7, 65, 79
  —single, 79
  double harness, 19
  dropper fly, 23
  fisherman's, 37
  fly, 67
  ground line, 44
  hammock, 42
  inside rolling, 42
  —orthodox, 42
  jam, 7
  kellig, 41, 44
  killick, 41
  lark's head, 33
  —mooring, 126
  lifting, 47
  lobster buoy, 35
  magnus, 41
  marline, 42
  midshipman's, 34
  net line, 44, 45
  ossel, 44
  ratline, 39
  reef pennant, 42
  ring, 35, 67, 79
  round turn mooring, 126
  sailor's, 33
  sampan, 37
  simple rope coil, 101
  —second method, 101
  single half, 33
  slingstone, 44
  slip, 34
  —halter, 42
  slipped, 3, 65
  slippery, 126
  stopper, 45
  —regular, 45
  studding-sail boom, 41
  swivel, 23
  tiller, 3
  timber, 41

  two half, 33
  —stopper, 45
  weaver's, 47
  well pipe, 47
Hitching
  closed fender, 119
  —open, 119
Hooks
  attaching a line, 67
  fastening an eye or bight, 73
  gorge, 131
  hitching shank, 69
  latch barb, 115
  making up, 13
  securing a line, 69
  --cod hooks to fishlines, 73
  snelled, 13
  wooden shafted, 117
Ice Fishing, 130
  second method, 131
Irons
  Arctic whaling, 115
  —one flued, 118
  --two flued, 118
  sperm whale, 115
  toggle, 118
Knots
  American shroud, 105
  barrel, 13
  —rolling, 65
  —twisted, 65
  blood, 25
  capstan, 34
  cinch, 44
  constrictor, 44
  crabber's eye, 55
  double English, 62
  double overhand, 23, 25
  double surgeon's, 21
  double water, 21
  —single, 21, 23
  dropper fly, 25
  eyed fly jam, 7
  figure-of-eight, 49
  fisherman's, 62
  —single, 11, 52
  —double, 81
  —fly, 69, 71
  —variation, 67
  ganging, 77, 81
  gill net, 79
  granny, 52
  grapevine, 62
  gut, 23
  hackamore, 53

Indian bridle, 53
ladder rung, 105
lineman's, 17
manharness, 19
Matthew Walker, 83
nonfriction, 39
ossel, 44
overhand, 49
—loop, 19
—sliding, 7
—trick chain, 107
pinch jam, 3
—triple turn, 7
reef, 3, 52, 165
—jamming, 69
—with bow, 52
return, 9
safety link, 9
shamrock, 53
single jury mast, 55
—double, 55
single cairnton, 9
snell, 25
Spanish, 55
square, 52
stevedore's, 52
tag, 67
theodore, 53
three-fold, 52
three-strand crown, 81
three-strand lanyard, 82
three-strand sennit, 85
three-strand single diamond, 83
three-strand single manrope, 82
—double, 82
three-strand single stopper, 82
—double, 82
three-strand star, 85
three-strand wall, 81
thumb, 49
tom fool's, 53
turtle, 11
twisted, 11
two-strand carrick diamond, 57
weaver's, 65
wemyss eyed fly, 9
wood, 9

Ladders
common rope, 105
—stern, 105

Lark's Heads
crossed, 34
double, 34
treble, 34

Lashings
Eskimo spear, 45
harpoon, 107
--second method, 109
rose, 125
wedding, 123

Leaders
attaching droppers, 25
—at right angles, 25
attaching line with angler's method, 27
—with figure-of-eight, 27
—with slip knot, 27
attaching snelled fly, 21
bending permanent loop in end of reel line, 79
round eye and square twist, 15
piano twist, 15

Litters
fisherman's, 75

Loops
adjustable leader, 21
angler's, 17
artillery, 19
attaching leader, 21
double water, 62
harness, 17
—double, 19
leader, 21, 23, 81
line, 21
lineman's, 17
multiple overhand knot, 19
overhand, 17
perfection, 21
permanent, 3
thumb knot, 17

Mats
Napoleon bend, 115
ocean plat weave, 115

Meshes
increasing, 169
reducing, 169

Meshing Gauges, 165

Meshing Needles or Shuttles, 165

Monkey Fists
crowned, 121
three-strand, 121
two-strand, 121

Mooring Lines
clove hitch, 126
securing, 126
—second method, 126

Nets
  brook hoop, 144
  circular, 113
  crab, 27
  fish, 169
  —with lock knot sheet bends, 169
  fyke, 133
  gill, 133
  hoop, 133
  landing, 171
  —standard, 181
  long tunnel pound, 144
  —short, 143
  set, 133
  shrimp, 107
  trammel, 133
  trap, 141
  —second method, 141
  tunnel, 133
Netting Shuttles or Needles
  filled shuttle, 147
  soldered wire shuttle, 147
  standard type, 147
Ornamental Designs
  sailor's breastplate, 55
Pointing
  common rope, 109
  needle hitched rope, 114
  ordinary eye, 111
  —rope, 111
Rattling Down, 118
Rules for Gill Nets, Mesh Measurements and Hanging Nets, 135
Seines
  straight, 135
  tapered, 135
Seizings
  flat, 99
  French, 101
  grapevine, 101
  inside clinch, 99
  —outside, 99
  middle, 101
  multiple wire, 13
  necklace, 101
  nippered, 100
  racking, 100
  round, 100
Sheepshanks
  man-o'-war, 60
  ordinary, 60
Shortenings
  overhand, 60

Slings
  bale, 123
  stage, 126
Snaking, 99
Spears
  fish, 131
  —second method, 131
Splices
  back, three-strand, 88
  —sailmaker's, 88
  chain, 94
  cut, 89
  eye, three-strand, 88
  —four-strand, 89
  —Flemish, 111
  —round thimble, 89
  —sailmaker's, 89
  —served, 89
  horseshoe, 94
  long, three-strand, 93
  short, three-strand, 89
  —sailmaker's, 91
Stoppers
  common, 127
  lark's head, 33
Strops
  selvage, 123
Swivels
  attaching gut, 15, 16
  attachment, 21
Taking a Rope Yarn Out of a Strand, 107
Ties
  attaching eyed fly, 11
  bowline, 23
  cinch, 9
  combination overhand knot, half hitch, 69
  constrictor knot, 9
  figure-of-eight, 3, 9
  —double, 9
  fisherman's knot, 69
  fishhook, 9, 67
  clove hitch, 67
  —common form, 69
  —French, 71
  —inside round turn, 7
  —multiple twist, 67
  —twist knot, 7
  —wedge, 9
  gut leader, 79
  jam knot, 3
  line connection, 39

line to swivel, 37, 39
lorn, 3
overhand, 3
round turn, 9
simple, 39
single sheet bend, 3
—with overhand knot, 3
turtle knot, 10

Traps
deep-water, 141
fish spear, 117
hoop net, 141
Lake Erie, 143
submarine, 143

Trawls
principle of construction, 75

Tricing in Two Ropes, 121

Turk's-heads
five-strand, 48
four-strand, 48
three-strand, 47

Walls
three-strand, 81

Weaving and Repairing Nets
formation of a meshing knot, 157
lengthening the chain, 151
net repairing, 157
patching a net, 163
trimming a tear, 155
weaving body of net, 152
—meshes, 147

Whippings
American, 96
fishline to hook, 71
—earlier method, 71
French, 97
grapevine, 97
herringbone, 99
ordinary, 96
palm and needle, 96
plain, 95
—in the middle of a line, 97
sailmaker's, 97
seaman's, 97
tackle, 27
temporary, 95

Worming, Parcelling and Serving, 114